D1527620

ELECTRA
A Gender Sensitive Study

ELECTRA

A Gender Sensitive Study of the Plays
(Aeschylus' *Oresteia* through Sam Shepard's
Curse of the Starving Class) Based on the Myth

BY BATYA CASPER LAKS

McFarland & Company, Inc., Publishers
Jefferson, North Carolina, and London

British Library Cataloguing-in-Publication data are available

Library of Congress Cataloguing-in-Publication Data

Laks, Batya Casper, 1942–
    Electra : a gender sensitive study of the plays (Aeschylus'
Oresteia through Sam Shepard's Curse of the starving class)
based on the myth / by Batya Casper Laks.
        p.   cm.
    ISBN 0-89950-924-X (lib. bdg. : 50# alk. paper) ∞
    1. Electra (Greek mythology) in literature.   2. Literature,
Modern — Greek influences.   I. Title.
PN57.E4B38   1995
809'.93351 — dc20   94-40306
                                                          CIP

Manufactured in the United States of America

McFarland & Company, Inc., Publishers
  Box 611, Jefferson, North Carolina 28640

To my father, in loving memory.
"Who loves peace and pursues peace.
Who loves humankind and draws them close to the law."
(*Proverbs of the Fathers*)

Table of Contents

Preface

This study examines various dramatic forms of *Electra*, one of the recurring myths of Western civilization. It defines the nature of the mythical complex and, except for two examples which I have included in the final chapter, in order to illustrate the modern writers' need to break with the myth (as with the guidelines of our rigidly hero-oriented, Western culture), it will include only those plays which conform to the same mythical deep structure.

In these plays, as in our culture so far, the hero is essentially male, and will be referred to, throughout, in the masculine. Throughout the text, when I use the word "man" I am referring not to humankind but to people of the male gender. I attempt, throughout, to make my language gender sensitive. Thematically, the feminine and the masculine, within this work, are presented as dramatic metaphors for the contradictory impulses that rage within the human soul: impulses for creativity, passion and freedom versus the drive of the "civilized" human being toward control, reason and order.

This book has afforded me enormous gratification in that it has allowed me to examine theater for what I believe is its authentic purpose: the dramatization of the human's deepest concerns and the inescapable confrontation of them with society.

I wish to thank the Department of Special Studies at the University of California–Los Angeles Library for making its resources available to me. I wish also to extend my gratitude to Carey Perloff for having generously furnished me with what was, at that time, an unpublished script of Ezra Pound's *Elektra*, together with the press releases for the world premiere of that play which she directed. I wish to thank Henry Goodman, now professor emeritus, UCLA Theater Department, for having inspired me, so many years ago, with his profound knowledge and with that open, friendly manner that is his trademark. My gratitude to Donald Cosentino, for having introduced me to and guided me so passionately through the powerful, mysterious world of myth. I am grateful to Carl Mueller who, with his abundant knowledge, has furnished me with some of the most exhilarating hours of my life, and I thank Anna Krayevska for her gentle friendship, and for her profound knowledge of the Greek texts. My most heartfelt thanks go to Susan Letzler Cole for her editorial skills — to Susan and David Cole both, for having lifted me from the abyss with the sheer joy of their intellects.

Above all I thank my children — for having believed in me.

Batya Casper Laks
March 1995

Introduction

And why should it be that whenever men [and women] have looked
for something solid on which to found their lives, they have chosen
not the facts in which the world abounds, but the myths of an immemorial imagination—preferring even to make life a hell for
themselves and their neighbors, in the name of some violent god, to
accepting gracefully the bounty the world affords?[1]

The issue raised in the above quotation will be the focus of this
book, which examines in its various dramatic forms a recurring myth
that is at the base of Western civilization. To that end it seems necessary
to question the nature of myth before attempting to assess its theatrical
form.

Claude Levi-Strauss claims that the oral tradition, which was the
original transmitter of mythical material, is like the work of *bricolage*.[2]
Like bricolage, it is often the result of a closed system in which the artist
is forced, over and over again, to reuse the same materials. Thus, in
folktales and in myth, songs, refrains, and specific lines are used
repeatedly in different forms, each time with a new dramatic intent.
The oral tradition, like bricolage, takes objects already imbued with
meaning through interactions they have had within other contexts and,
with them, makes new formations, thereby creating yet again new ar-
rangements of meaning. The results of bricolage and myth are similar
to the results of theater. Medieval performances, for example, by means
of the naive and spontaneous participation of acrobateurs, jongleurs,
and devils, together with the interaction of all the above with the audience, produced theater that had a far different and greater impact than
had been foreseen by the church-writers at the outset.

Levi-Strauss claims that a myth is comprised of all of its variants
including its latest interpretation.[3] Again, the significance lies in the
bricolage effect. Each new form of the myth is encrusted not only with
the legacy of the past and the special significance it had for its initial
audience, but with the specific relevance and social commentary that
it has for the present. The post–Freudian world is incapable of
understanding the ancient Greek myths in the way that the Greek
world had, but rather, in a way that combines what we believe to be the

Isis Suckling Horus. Aegyptisches Museum, Staatliche Museen, Berlin. Photo: Foto Marburg / Art Resource, New York.

fifth-century Athenian understanding of the myth with our own Freudian and post–Freudian perspectives.

Myth is part of the oral tradition and as such its nature depends on its fluidity, its essential changeability from performance to performance, and its independence of the written form. The magic of the Electra myth consists in this very fluidity, in the fact that it is never trapped within any specific dramatic form, but appears again and again, each time with a different face and for a different effect. The oral tradition which constituted the original conveyor of the myth was and is to this day Aristotelian by nature. It is mimetic, an imitation of reality. But the myth that it conveys deal simultaneously with the real and the ideal. It transforms the social into narrative, the punctual into the durative, the diachronic into the synchronic. It exists in two simultaneous time spaces: at the moment of presentation and for all time. Prime examples of this duality can be found in the myths of the Passover and the Easter stories. Theodor Gaster sees myth as interdependent with ritual and, as such, as a form that has a close affinity to drama.[4] Indeed, we see this to be the case with the ceremonial enactments of the Easter and the Passover myths. However, the tale within which the myth is couched is always based upon the immediate and the specific, fabricated as with bricolage from the structure and complexities of contemporary society. Gaster defines myth as "any presentation of the actual in terms of the ideal."[5] T. S. Eliot also said that all our realities are founded in concretes and it is up to us to come up with interpretations.[6] This view of myth coincides exactly with the understanding of theater that will be explored in this book, a theater which is, after all, the conveyor of a myth in its multiple forms. The universal is derived, by theater-goers, from the specific.

Gaster describes the evolution of the mythical in the following way: first is the "primitive stage" in which "the story is the direct accompaniment of a ritual performed for purely pragmatic purposes, and it serves to present the several features of that ritual . . . as incidents in a transcendental situation." Today we might consider the *Passover ceremony* or the Easter Mass, in which myth and ritual are intrinsically related, as examples of this stage. Second is the "dramatic stage" in which "the ritual or cultic performance has . . . been toned down into an actual pantomimic representation of the story," such as the Mystery Plays which are no longer myths. Then comes the "liturgical stage" in which the story no longer parallels the ritual, but is simply a recitation, a religious ceremony, such as the medieval Christian hymns which are only a part of the ritual. Finally there is the "literary stage . . . a mere tale, severed altogether from any ritual observance."[7] Gaster gives the Homeric hymns and some of the Hebrew psalms as examples of this stage. In fact, it seems that the myth is none of the above, but that which operates both synchronically and diachronically, as does the theater that we shall observe in this study.

Electra is one of the most recurring myths of Western civilization. This book will attempt to define the nature of its mythical complex and illustrate how all the plays under examination—except those whose deviations from the structure I regard as a deliberate attempt on the part of the playwright to change the myth—are comprised of the same mythical deep-structure.

Myth became incorporated into Western theater for the first time in fifth-century Athens when both the mythical content and the dramatic form constituted a reflection of the contemporary social structure and a record of the changing ideologies particular to that society. In Jacobean England—two thousand years after the Greek period—a mythical complex that conforms to the deep-structure of the Greek Electra myth can be discerned (albeit in a very different theatrical form) within Shakespeare's *Hamlet*. It is the resurfacing of the Electra myth within a social structure that bears uncanny points of resemblance to that of classical Greece. Yet again in twentieth-century Europe we shall see the myth reappear and flourish as the result of an intellectual impulse similar to that which had given rise to the plays of classical Greece.

Claude Levi-Strauss claims that though the surface structure might differ radically from presentation to presentation, myths can be classified and recognized as belonging to the same group by means of the invariable pattern of their deep-structure.[8] Thus, though the surface structure, the theatrical treatment, and the ensuing sociopolitical messages differ drastically from play to play, the deep-structure remains invariable throughout all the Electra myths within this study except for those plays that I will examine as deliberate attempts on the part of the playwrights to change the mythical structure. The plays that I will be examining as typical of the myth share all of the main five characters. They all present an Agamemnon figure that has been replaced in some way by Aegisthus, and they all have an Aegisthus that has usurped the position of Agamemnon both in the political arena and in the affections of the Queen. In all of these plays there is a Clytemnestra figure whose affections are diverted from her children and directed toward the present ruler. Electra is always the unmated, the imprisoned and the vengeful, and Orestes is, in all the plays, the son and heir of Agamemnon and the would-be avenger of his father's murder.

In the myth Orestes always approaches the action from a separate physical or psychological space from that of the other characters. He is always forced to take a stand against the establishment. The focal point of action is always the meeting of the old (Agamemnon) with the new (Orestes) and the play is always propelled into action by the meeting of the male (Orestes) with the female (Electra). Electra represents filial loyalty, Clytemnestra is "tainted," a mother manquée, and Aegisthus is characterized by a lack of idealism or any sense of the spiritual.

In *The Myth of the Eternal Return*, Mircea Eliade[9] describes archaic times as a period of ahistoricity in which men and women, unequipped to rationalize the harshness of human suffering in terms of history and human cause and effect, used ritual as a safeguard of time as circular, static and recognizable. Ritual celebrations of the cycle of seasons, of death and rebirth, always reenacted the same point in time, always brought men and women back to the pattern of life and death that has always been and will never change.

Eliade claims that the ancient Hebrews were the first to propel men and women into a sense of history with their understanding that political and social defeats and victories were caused directly and deliberately by divine intervention.

However that may be, Aristotelian logic soon replaced the instinctually recognizable cycle of the eternal return with the cause and effect of a homocentric world.

Only in post–Hegelian times have people become disenchanted with history. Only with Nietzsche did thinkers begin to question the validity of the Judao-Christian heritage and hark back to static, prepatriarchal times and to the myth of the eternal return as an alternative to the masculine, the causative and the destructive.

Nietzsche knew that the twentieth century would have to question. He knew that it would be a period of constantly changing and struggling ideologies.

The Electra myth, I believe, originated out of an archaic myth of eternal return. The purpose of this book is to examine its adaptation into the early patriarchal system, to examine its transformation from its earliest known forms in Aeschylus, Sophocles, and Euripides, and to observe its manipulation in the hands of subsequent writers.

These Greek plays always took place at the festival of Dionysus, a theater dedicated specifically to the celebration of the cyclical myth of return, for just as early Christians in the Middle Ages clung to pagan images and ideals, so early Greek patriarchs clung to the archaic concept of static time.

Geza Roheim, in the *Gates of the Dream*, identifies two sources of mythology: the "dream" and "the problem of growing up."[10]

Ancient Greek mystery rites were ceremonies that led the adolescent through a symbolic death and rebirth as preparation for adulthood. Anthropological sources for many cultures testify to the fact that adolescent boys were — and in some instances still are — removed from the comfort of the maternal into an all-male society beyond the confines of the homestead. Only when fully initiated into the rites of manhood can they return as beneficial members of society. In all the plays included in this study as those that conform to the deep-structure of the myth, the audience witnesses the rebirth of Orestes. He is an adolescent returning to his community from a separate space. As such, he is similar to the actor, the prophet, and the hero. All such figures come home from an off-stage space, all such figures grapple with their vision and are ultimately snared within the too-close emotional ties of their own homes. Within this context, the hero is always male.

In all these versions of the Electra myth there has been an artificial separation of the male from the female. The plays of Sophocles and Euripedes seem to be deliberate dramatizations of the danger that the artificial divorce of the sexes in Athenian society had upon its culture.

The enormous contradiction between the secondary status of women in fifth-century Athens, women who were bought as child-brides away from their mothers' homes and left voiceless and without status from that point on within an enclosed women's house, and the larger-than-life amazons of classical Greek mythology would indicate an exaggerated fear that the men of that period must have had of women and female sexuality, and an overpowering need on the part of men to suppress women.

It is not surprising that this fear and opposition of the sexes should surface as part of the inner structure of this myth. It is my belief that in archaic times this myth had recorded the murder of the male by the matriarch and the incorporation of his body into the mother earth for the purpose of fertility. In patriarchal hands, the focus of the murder becomes primarily that of the female (mother) by the avenging male (son), itself the story of what many believe was the patriarchal takeover of earlier female goddesses. The story then becomes that of the repressed female (Electra) as emblem of the repressed emotional life of a people and its desperate attempt to be liberated and incorporated into some vision of the future. More than likely, Sophocles and Euripedes were both warning their generation of the violence that would ensue as the result of the artificial separation of the male and female principles within the Athenian male.

In its outlook and treatment of women, the Jacobean period bears striking similarities to fifth-century Athens. Texts from the Jacobean period record the accepted societal policy regarding women, the necessity that they be modest, acquiescent, temperate, pious, and chaste, and that they have no voice in politics, religion, or the education of their children. Yet, as with the Greeks, the women of the Jacobean theater are noted for their fiery temperaments, their intemperate sexuality and their proclivity for lust, murder and insanity. The Jacobean period was also a period of vast expansionism, of rapidly changing ideologies and of gross materialism; hence it is understandable that a visionary such as Shakespeare could create *Hamlet*, a play which adheres to all the aspects of the deep-structure of the Electra myth. It might also be argued that Shakespeare was consciously writing during England's adolescence (in which case the theme and structure of the Electra play would be particularly appropriate) and warning England both of its enormous potential for idealism, for the Hamlet/Orestean vision, and of the danger that it might succumb to the short-sighted materialism of its Aegisthean complacence.

The end of the nineteenth century sought an alternative to the patriarchal legacy of Western culture, and the task of the early years of this century became for many the creation of a new history. I will examine the Electra plays of this century as works which confront the status quo with the new, sometimes deliberately aheroic, Orestean vision. I will examine the anticlassical, antitragic, antiheroic structure of modern theater and the expression of the ideology of each play in terms of its theatrical space, structure, use of images and language.

Levi-Strauss describes the human need to stratify existence in terms of clusters of similarities and binary oppositions.[11] Western culture recognizes its own experience in terms of:

male/female	logical/instinctual
spiritual/material	day/night
rational/emotional	repression/freedom.

All these oppositions are manipulated again and again within the theatrical configurations of the Electra myth. Patriarchal history has become associated with action, with Apollonian logic and masculine repression, whereas the archaic world represents static female acquiescence, nature, instinctual wisdom and patience. Electra is heroic in her relentless loyalty to past values and if she is violent, ruthless and even insane it is because she has become the hysterical call for the deliverance of the imprisoned female and life-force. I will demonstrate how already in the Greek plays Electra evolves from the female priestess, instrument of ritual and renewal (Aeschylus), to the "insane" voice of the antiestablishment (Sophocles), to the pathetic call of the demented, imprisoned female spirit (Euripides). Yet, where Orestes is the hope for the future, Electra is the only one who understands the values of the past and who clings tenaciously to them throughout the long centuries of patriarchal culture. She will spin herself out or relinquish her hold only with the Orestean promise of change. As with the ancient Greeks and the Jacobeans, the twentieth century is characterized by its extreme violence, by expansionism, contradictory absolutist ideologies, warfare, cruelty, gross materialism and periodic bouts of idealistic fervor.

It is at periods of changing and conflicting ideologies, when the Orestean hero appears as he who struggles to take his generation out of the myopic and repressive materialism typified by Aegisthus and move it toward the ideal of the Orestean vision, that the myth of Electra is reexamined. Such a reexamination was dramatized when the religious confidence of the High Renaissance crumbled into the materialism and the uncertainty of the Jacobean period. It is dramatized, over and over again, within the changing ideologies of our own century.

Peter Brook describes theater as that of "the invisible-made-visible."[12] The plays within this study manifest fundamental problems of contemporary Western society as well as those of fifth-century Athens. For the duration of the theatrical performance, each play actualizes the imagined and the intuited into physical reality on stage. As such, each becomes a ritual binding of players and spectators in a shared materialization of abstractions that are germane to its respective time-period. These plays concretize the most dire problems of Western society: the psychological and political rift caused by the artificial separation of the male and the female principles within the culture and the violence that this has engendered; the development and progression of such concepts as honor, justice, patriotism and vengeance versus morality and the individual conscience; the development and gradual transformation of the community's understanding of the "tragic" and the "heroic," both in theatrical structure and in content; and the issue of "sanity" as a characteristic that becomes the "party line," while "insanity" becomes the voice of the individual contradicting that of the establishment. The tragic hero is defined as the harbinger of a new moral code, and these plays become the struggle of the hero to coopt the world that is foisted upon him toward his own revolutionary vision.

I

Prehistory

In all areas of the known world, from prehistoric findings to primitive sketches of today's preschool children, images of the circle, specifically of the snake devouring its own tail, abound. What is the significance of such a recurring motif? Erich Neumann writes:

> ... the *uroboros*, the circular snake biting its tail, is the symbol of the psychic state of the beginning, of the original situation, in which man's consciousness and ego were still small and undeveloped. As symbol of the origin and of the opposites contained in it, the *uroboros* is the "Great Round," in which positive and negative, male and female, elements of consciousness, elements hostile to consciousness, and unconscious elements are intermingled. In this sense the *uroboros* is also a symbol of a state in which chaos, the unconscious, and the psyche as a whole were undifferentiated—and which is experienced by the ego as a borderline state.[13]

The earliest, preconscious state of the human being is symbolized for us within the prehistoric image of the protective *uroboros*, the enclosed, womb-like circle of the snake devouring its own tail, image of the eternal union of the male with the female. The *uroboros* is a state at rest. In it all oppositions coalesce. It is a state characteristic of the predawn of human history, and it is a state that is recreated with each nursing mother and child.

Despite its essential harmony of opposites, the uroboros is characteristically feminine in nature, for it is the female start that is inert, elementary and conservative. But with the growth of the human consciousness, the emerging individual experiences his or her earliest and most traumatic form of rejection, a rejection that is brought about by the withdrawal of the lifeline, the milk and comfort of the mother. With this sudden withdrawal of immediate comfort, all oppositions suddenly attack the consciousness. Hunger is experienced instead of food; want instead of comfort; more devastating than anything else, loneliness is experienced where earlier the only sensation had been that of containment and the centeredness characteristic of the "participation mystique." This state of loneliness and rejection is expressed in myths and folktales as exile and as the lonely expanses of desert. It is the essential precondition for consciousness and the human voyage towards maturation, both on an individual and on a societal level. Thus, it is in the desert that heroes and leaders from Abraham, Moses, Jesus, and Mohammed have realized their vision. (Throughout this study we have to bear in mind that Western history has been, for the most part, a record of men and women—as understood and portrayed by men—in a postprimitive, patriarchal world. Hence we have no authentic insights into the soul-searchings of the women of ancient times, and no accounts whatsoever of the spiritual awakenings of ancient women-warriors. As Carol Gilligan says in her book, *In a Different Voice*: "It all goes back, of course, to Adam and Eve." "It" could be said to mean the problems caused by an all-male interpretation of human development. Gilligan says that "if you make a woman out of a man, you are bound to get into trouble. In the life cycle, as in the Garden of Eden, the woman has been the deviant."[14])

However, Erich Neumann claims that the hero represents more than the individual male: "The hero," he says,

> is the archetypal forerunner of mankind in general. His fate is the pattern in accordance with which the masses of humanity must live, and always have lived, however haltingly and distantly; and however short of the ideal man they have fallen, the stages of the hero myth have become constituent elements in the personal development of every individual.[15]

It is in the lonely regions of the desert that the emerging male first confronts his spirituality, a state that is the antitheses of the physical and the inert that have become so associated with the female. The female retains the characteristics of the Great Mother, container of all life. Thus she is depicted in early civilizations as the vessel, the dark interior of which is life-producing, nurturing and also threatening by means of its mystery and its ability to hold, ensnare and destroy. The darkness within the Mother Vessel is the night of the unconscious mind. Neumann makes the point that people still today talk of "inwardness" and of one's "inner," more reflective qualities. He maintains that this is because people have, from earliest times, projected themselves onto the "world vessel" by which they are encompassed.

Thus it is believed that the earliest forms of human experience failed to distinguish between the masculine and the feminine, for all aspects of reality were subsumed at the predawn of human consciousness within an enveloping obscurity akin to the preconscious state of the infant within the mother's womb. One of the earliest myths of ancient Egypt depicts the human being's first, tentative attempt at self-definition, for it portrays the young hero "Shu" separating the sky from the earth. Ancient Egyptians regarded Nut — the sky — as feminine, perhaps because objective reality was still experienced as all-encompassing, because the human being saw him or herself as an embryo within a womb-like world.

An early Maori creation myth, on the other hand, is one of many that identified the heavens as the masculine and the spiritual:

> ... Tane-mahuta, the god and father of forests, of birds, and of insects, arose and struggled with his parents; in vain with hands and arms he strove to rend them apart. He paused; firmly he planted his head on his mother Papa, the earth, and his feet he raised up against his father Rangi, the sky; he strained his back and his limbs in a mighty effort. Now were rent apart Rangi and Papa, and with reproaches and groans of woe they cried aloud: "Wherefore do you thus slay your parents? ... But Tane-mahuta ... regarded not their cries and their groans; far, far beneath him he pressed down Papa, the earth; far, far above him ... he thrust up Rangi, the sky ... so that they were rent apart, and darkness was made manifest, and light made manifest also.[16]

The separation of the world parents constitutes the birth of human consciousness and with it ensue the ambivalence and the guilt of human experience:

> In the view of the cabala, original sin consisted essentially in this: that damage was done to the Deity. Concerning the nature of this damage there are various views. The most widely accepted is that the First Man, Adam Kadmon, made a division between King and Queen, and that he sundered the Shekhina from union with her spouse, and from the whole hierarchy of the Sephiroth.[17]

In early consciousness (to be distinguished from the human being's preconscious state) earth is experienced as the all-encompassing Mother Nature. The human creature is tied to her for life, for nurture and for sustenance. The sky, on the other hand, represents a "masculine" world of aspirations, of strife that is essential for the maturity and the self-differentiation of the individual. Spirituality as part of the masculine (sky) experience becomes recognizable in the maturing male adolescent, as in the early development of civilization, only after the essential wrench from the womb-like, nurturing, but ultimately stifling Earth Mother has been initiated.

It is believed that for several thousands of years the human being failed to make the connection between copulation and fertilization and in many areas of the world women were worshipped as the divine producers of life and, as such, as the sole force of immortality. Even after man's function in the process of reproduction was understood, the woman's ability to carry, bear and nurture human life accorded her a position of veneration within the community of men. We see from prehistoric art and totemic practice (even from art as late as some of the early portrayals of the Virgin Mary) that women were believed to have conceived by means of totemic (or divine) spirit. In fact, the original meaning of the word "virgin" did not refer to a chaste woman but to a woman who was emotionally independent of men, who, while perhaps physically fertilized by human sperm, was spiritually impregnated by a life-engendering force. In her book, *The Woman's Encyclopedia of Myths and Secrets*, Barbara G. Walker claims that

> Mary's impregnation was similar to Persephone's. In her Virgin guise, Persephone sat in a holy cave and began to weave the great tapestry of the universe, when Zeus appeared as a phallic serpent, to beget the savior Dionysus on her. Mary sat in the temple and began to spin a blood-red thread, representing Life in the tapestry of fate, when the angel Gabriel "came in unto her" (Luke 1:28), . . . Gabriel's name means literally "divine husband."[18]

Prehistoric notions of the earth as the source of life and death were closely related to the human experience of vegetable life and its succession of seasons. Prehistoric art and ritual suggest that people at the dawn of human history saw a connection between the fecundating powers of blood in the woman's menstrual cycle and in pregnancy and the need for the fertilization of nature. It seems that early mother goddesses needed human blood in order to fertilize the earth and ensure the rebirth of nature each spring. Primitive art testifies to early rituals in which the mother goddess sacrificed her physical partner after having become impregnated by him. The same art also demonstrates a symbolic connection between the mother goddess and the bee (the queen bee also kills the male after coitus). Archaeological findings indicate the existence of prehistoric annual kings who were slaughtered each winter and whose bodies were torn asunder and scattered over the dry earth, whose blood was poured into the earth to ensure the renewal of life in the spring. Early tombs with funnels within them for the conveyance of libations to the bodies of the dead have been found. Possibly, these libations were the blood and the food, necessary for the rebirth of nature.

The infant is inseparable from the body of his or her mother, dependent upon her for his or her life's blood (milk). With maturity, it becomes essential for the child to make a psychological and physical break with the mother. So it was, in the dawn of human consciousness, that the human creature was at one with, attached and dependent upon the great mother, Mother Earth. Early Egyptian findings quite clearly depict the young god as part of the mother goddess. She is his throne. He sits and rules on her. He is killed by her and becomes incorporated into her. He is physically and psychologically part of her. Osiris is murdered and buried in the trunk of a tree (hence, suggests Neumann, the tree and the coffin become symbols of life, death and resurrection) and is ultimately liberated from there by his sister-lover. Death and resurrection as enacted by the gods are the theme of nature itself.

Conversely, early art and philosophy portray spirituality as the "father." The father, as such, represents the longed-for emancipation from the female — the self-realization of the human being.

In his analysis of human consciousness, Neumann makes a distinction between the personal and the "suprapersonal" parents of the hero:

> The fact that the hero has two fathers and two mothers is a central feature in the canon of the hero myth. Besides his personal father there is a "higher," that is to say an archetypal, father figure, and similarly an archetypal mother figure appears beside the personal mother. This double descent, with its contrasted personal and suprapersonal parental figures, constellates the drama of the hero's life.[19]

(Again when referring to the maturation of the individual, or to the development of the hero as archetype, the scholar addresses himself only to the male child.) A boy's personal father represents tradition, reactionism, authority. The hero is the adolescent who pits himself against the old values as represented by the personal father, inspired by the ideals, the liberal, visionary message of the forward-looking spirit, represented by the Supra or Transpersonal Father. Thus, the successful hero undergoes two vital struggles before he embarks upon his heroic journey to full manhood: the first against his earthbound, all-consuming, deadly, Terrible Mother; the second against the reactionary, tradition-oriented Personal Father. In the myth of Orestes from Aeschylus onward, the hero, moved by the spirit of his dead, suprapersonal father, struggles first to destroy the murderous Clytemnestra and then Aegisthus, the materialistic and oppressive imposter king.

In freeing himself from the Terrible Mother, the hero enfranchises himself from the earthbound and the regressive within his own personality. Only when the hero recognizes himself as a separate entity from the world around him can he dispel the threat to his personal well-being of the feminine and the nurturing. Thus it is at this stage, in ancient myths, that images of the friendly, female, sister-lover emerge. Electra is such a figure. She is the sister-lover of the young hero and represents corporal reality. Athena is also such a figure, she is a benign goddess and, as such, represents the realm of the spirit.

To my mind the original myth of Electra was just such an expression of early man's struggle toward spiritual growth and independence and the subsequent plays that built upon the myth have become re-examinations of that struggle in its different forms.

This would explain the prevalence of incest in many versions of the Electra myth as the struggle of a hero torn between the dualities within his own nature, and the neurotically close family ties in which it is not always quite clear where one family member ends and the other begins, depicting man as a complex being and as an integral part of an all-too close social structure. When Aristotle maintained that the most tragic situations are those which involve close family members, he was aware that blood knots draw upon the deepest wells of the human unconscious.

Aeschylus: *The Libation Bearers* (458 B.C.)

Aeschylus' Clytemnestra bears an uncanny similarity to the many prehistoric mother goddesses who sacrificed their partners to their magical powers of fertility and destruction and were virgin-like in their independence of their mates. Is Aeschylus deliberately manipulating his audience's dim memories of such rites as a means of drawing them under the spell of his theater as, for example, in *Agamemnon* when Clytemnestra appears to the spectators drenched in her husband's blood after she has murdered him?

CLYTEMNESTRA

So he goes down, and the life is bursting out of him —
great sprays of blood, and the murderous shower
wounds me, dyes me black and I, I revel
like the Earth when the spring rains come down,
the blessed gifts of god, and the new green spear
splits the sheath and rips to birth in glory![20]

Aeschylus' Agamemnon is reminiscent of ancient fertilizing god-kings that were sacrificed and buried to ensure the rebirth of nature, while his Orestes is the universal youth determined to rid himself of the dragon of maternal oppression and in so doing to liberate Electra, the imprisoned life-force within him. Aeschylus provides an easy way out for such adolescent rebellion. In his trilogy which deals with the oppositions within human experience, the male, the female, the spiritual and the physical conspire to bring about psychological harmony and social balance. Is it possible that both Aeschylus and his audience were building, within this play of social reform, upon a shared memory of ancient goddesses and fertility rites, that Aeschylus was deliberately utilizing the religious ceremony of the Dionysian festival as a means of drawing his spectators into a meeting of old and new ideologies for his lesson of order and rebellion, freedom and restraint?

For *The Libation Bearers*, the central play of Aeschylus' trilogy, the ancient Greek audience is congregated around a circular space of pounded earth. In the center of this circle, at the focal point of attention, is the burial mound of the dead king, Agamemnon. All attention is focused on this spot as Electra and the chorus of slave women draw toward it with song and dance to fertilize the mound of Agamemnon's grave with libations of wine (blood) and tears.

ELECTRA

And I will tip libations to the dead.
I call out to my father. Pity me,
    dear Orestes too.
Rekindle the light that saves our house!
. . . .
        Bring up your blessings,
Up into the air . . . [183].

Electra and the women pour libations (and tears) into the earth:

ELECTRA

Father,
you have it now, the earth has drunk your wine [184].

And in a magnificently economical piece of drama, Electra walks in the footsteps of her brother (which are identical to her own) until she is suddenly confronted by the appearance — almost the apparition — of Orestes himself. In the mere span of a few stanzas, Electra has poured the libation, sewn the seed and has conjured up "a mighty tree" (187),

new life from the old. Orestes is the resurrected Agamemnon. According to Jan Kott, he is also the actualized Electra, for Kott claims that
the prehero state of Orestes has been dramatically represented here, on
stage, as a female.[21] The mature hero, the fully realized hero is conjured up by Electra and emerges before us fully armed in masculine
form. In theatrical terms, Orestes is represented as the self-differenti-
ated Electra. The Greek hero is here the male that has emerged from
the chrysalis of the female.

The entire first part of the play is the goading into action of Electra
and Orestes by the chorus. In Macbethian fashion the chorus chants:

CHORUS

"Word for word, curse for curse
be born now," Justice thunders,
    hungry for retribution,
"stroke for bloody stroke be paid.
    The one who acts must suffer."
Three generations strong the word resounds [192].

The chorus first goads Electra into calling upon the gods for vengeance,
it then rouses both Electra and Orestes into a veritable religious ecstasy
for vengeance and murder, a holy war:

CHORUS

Now our comrades group underground.
Our masters' wreaking hands are doomed— [194].

This vengeance is the justice of the ancient Near East, an eye for an eye.
It is the justice of the old warlords, founders and destroyers of the house
of Atreus. The chorus sings, "What can redeem the blood that wets the
soil?" (179). At the grave site, Electra cries to the spirit of her father:

ELECTRA

Your grave receives a girl in prayer
and a man in flight, and we are one,
    and the pain is equal, whose is worse?
And who outwrestles death— . . . ? [193].

For us, this image might evoke the biblical one of Jacob wrestling with
the angel (Genesis), for Electra and Orestes are mythically one. Electra
perhaps is the birth of the hero, and Orestes, the "mighty tree," image
of resurrection and full manhood. The chorus hails the coming of
Orestes with the words:

CHORUS

Look, the light is breaking!
The huge chain that curbed the halls gives way.
Rise up, proud house, long, too long
your walls lay fallen, strewn along the earth [220].

The central action of *The Libation Bearers* seems to support William Ridgeway's theory that Greek tragedy emerged initially from pre–Dionysian mimetic dances, enacted in order to evoke the protective spirits of dead heros upon the living.[22] Whether or not we accept this idea, we do believe that tragedies were originally religious ceremonies. The burial mound, the ritual pouring of libations and the evocation of the spirit of the dead Agamemnon constitute the core and mainstay of *The Libation Bearers*. It is essential for the religious, if not the hypnotic appeal of this drama, that the burial mound of the dead king be center stage. For the purpose of this ritual, this spot represents the center of the earth, the mound upon which the archetypal hero (Adam, Jesus, Mohammed) is born. At center stage it represents the hero's voyage to the source of insight and the actor's journey to his source of imagination.

In *Myth of the Eternal Return*, Mircea Eliade claims that to the archaic mind every significant human action was a repetition of a divine act. Moreover, it was a repetition of the act of original creation. He claims that in prehistoric times deeds gained mythical significance by virtue of their repetition:

> . . . an object or an act becomes real only insofar as it imitates or repeats an archetype. Thus, reality is acquired solely through repetition or participation; everything which lacks an exemplary model is "meaningless," i.e., it lacks reality.[23]

It seems significant that for the plays in which Aeschylus moves toward law and order he chooses actions that imitate those of the early Greek creation myths: the violent overthrow of the old masculine order for the instigation of the new. The first mythic recording of the Orestes story is found in Homer's *Odyssey*, which tells only of the virtuous, vengeful murder of Aegisthus by Orestes.[24] Aeschylus seems to have introduced a novel twist to the traditional myth of Orestes for the purpose of his drama, for his trilogy is no longer merely the record of patriarchal takeover, of the son surpassing or defending the father figure, the supreme male, in order to gain manhood, rather it is the story of matricide, of the overthrow of the mother goddess. It is ultimately the instigation, in dramatic form, of the patriarchal system itself.

The dramatic innovations of Aeschylus revolutionize the myth and, as Levi-Strauss claims, myth is comprised of all of its variations.[25]

As we have just noted, Aeschylus is the first known writer to introduce female characters as forces within the myth of Orestes. It is Aeschylus who first portrays Clytemnestra as a dramatic figure, indeed, as a powerful, crazed, frustrated and wronged woman, and it is he who for the first time introduces an Electra, a second female character, to become the central figure of his drama. In effect, Aeschylus' "significant action," his "act of creation" (as defined by Eliade) constitutes the act of female rebellion. It dramatizes the revolutionary potential of frustrated and entrapped women and this rebellion is granted mythical status in the eyes of the spectators because it builds upon the ancient images of mother goddesses and fertility cults and upon their awareness of mystery cults which were still popular in Greece at that time.

It is believed that Aeschylus was playing to a sexually segregated, repressively patriarchal society, yet he was doing so in celebration of Dionysus, a mystery god, god of women, of frenzy and of chaotic sexual freedom, a god that epitomized as did none other the greatest threat to the reason-loving Athenian male, a deity that represented the antithesis of Athenian, masculine shrewdness, heroic excellence (*arete*), public law and social order. Eliade claims that

> A sacrifice . . . not only exactly reproduces the initial sacrifice revealed by a god *ab origine*, at the beginning of time, it also takes place at that same primordial mythical moment. . . .

He writes that

> . . . every sacrifice repeats the initial sacrifice and coincides with it. All sacrifices are performed at the same mythical instant of the beginning; through the paradox of rite, profane time and duration are suspended. And the same holds true for all repetitions, i.e. all imitations of archetypes; through such imitation, man is projected into the mythical epoch in which the archetypes were first revealed. . . . The abolition of profane time and the individual's projection into mythical time do not occur, of course, except at essential periods— those, that is, when the individual is truly himself: on the occasion of rituals or of important acts. . . .[26]

If we accept Eliade's theory of the relevance of time to the archaic mind it becomes easier for us to imagine the powerful hold that Aeschylus' theater must have had over his audience. *The Oresteia* was no isolated work. In the eyes of the spectators it built upon the creation of the world. It was fabricated out of the themes and memories of the earliest deities, creation myths and rites and the sacrifices that it depicted, both of life and of conscience, became embossed for them as they watched, with the mythical fullness of the sacrifice *ab origine*:

> . . . insofar as an act (or an object) acquires a certain reality through repetition of certain paradigmatic gestures, . . . there is an implicit abolition of profane time, of duration, of "history"; and he who reproduces the exemplary gesture thus finds himself transported into the mythical epoch in which its revelation took place.[27]

Herbert Blau refers to the meeting of Orestes and Electra over the tomb of their father. He says:

> All theory of theater converges there. That's where the real acting takes place. "Are you alive? Where are you living? What *is* your life" When we speak of what Stanislavski called Presence in acting, we must also speak of its Absence, the dimensionality of time through the act, the fact that he who is performing can die there in front of your eyes; is in fact doing so. Of all the performing arts, the theater stinks most of mortality. Buber said of Hasidism that it is "the only mysticism in which *time* is hallowed" somewhere "on the borderland of faith where the soul draws breath between word and word." It is a superb definition of what theater should be. The secret of any craft is mastery of time.[28]

With this in mind the full significance of the festival of Dionysus and of the Electra plays becomes clearer: Aeschylus' theater is part of time itself. It is neither more nor less than the current chapter in an ongoing creation myth, a particular moment in an eternal reckoning, a self-assessment that is by nature religious, social, and political, a questioning that was initiated at the dawn of human consciousness — by the initial separation of the world parents, heaven and earth — and that will last until the end of human time. Aeschylus' work forms a part of those very creation myths that record the human being's struggle toward consciousness. It is an enactment of the very first human sacrifice, a human attempt to be aware, to be in control, and — above all — to be "heroic."

Eliade also presents his understanding of the significance of place for the archaic mind. A place becomes a sacred center of the universe by means of the significance of the action, of the sacrifice that is enacted thereon. Jerusalem as a reflection of its heavenly counterpart or Mount Tabor (in the worth of Israel) as the biblical navel of the earth constitute only two examples of a whole host of traditions that regard the significant acts of creation and of their cultures as having occurred at the center of the world. In fact, Medieval theater dramatically manipulated the cultural promise that chosen man from Adam to Christ rose and fell on the identical spot, a place sanctified by the repetition of meaningful action, and the center of the medieval stage also became intensified by the accumulated significance of the creation of the world, the births of Adam and of Eve, their banishment from Eden, the birth, crucifixion and resurrection of Christ and the final judgment and deliverance of mankind.

The theater is such a center, and the cyclical repetitions of meaningful actions upon this center spot themselves become a source of myth, for with each repeated act of creation, with each repeated human sacrifice, the sanctity of the theatrical center is intensified. Thus, quite apart from the religious connotations of the festival of Dionysus, the very act of gathering annually around the circular arena becomes a ritual of return. Each return adds mythical depth and heightened meaning for the spectators. The center spot of the stage, at the moment of the performance, at the gathering of the populace, is charged with the sanctity of myth.

In *The Libation Bearers*, Aegisthus assumes the figure of the hero's Personal Father. His is the voice of reactionism and constraint and he stands in the way of Orestes' advancement. On the other hand, the spirit of Agamemnon within the burial mound has become over the years of Orestes' absence from Argos the source and fountainhead of all Orestes' aspirations. Yet only by eradicating the maternal can Orestes reach his goal. Such is the dragon that this hero has to slay, which might well prove a prototype for all heroic trials. In some sense, Orestes' trial is experienced simultaneously by the four thousand Greeks who attend this theater. Such is the myth and the ritual which is enacted here within the theater of Aeschylus and the subsequent playwrights in our study.

As the shaman travels imaginatively outward toward his fountain of creativity and returns from there to make physical the imagined on stage for his audience, and as the adolescent groping toward manhood journeys outward in his rite-of-passage from the community to confront his greatest fear and returns as a benefactor of his society, so the Greek tragic actor and the Greek hero draw their creative spirits from a separate space and are inspired into action, ultimately, from the depths of the sacred burial mound. In such a spirit Orestes is exiled from his immediate community and returns to confront the challenge of his own manhood within the community of gathered Athenians, at the burial mound of his father. All action emanates from this burial mound. The spectators surround the action physically and emotionally in a gigantic circle creating between themselves and the actors one closed centrifugal circuit of action and intensity. The audience, pulled magnetically to the spirit of the dead king, is held there by a shared, half-remembered, half-intuited sense of the rite of death and rebirth and by a communal need to evoke the heroic within their midst. The action in Aeschylus' trilogy has become not merely the evocation of the benign spirit of the dead king but the dramatic transition of one generation to the next. It is the blessing of the old for the new and it recreates, in physical form, the blessing of the gods upon the spectators and their own contemporary vision of heroism.

This play bears little resemblance to any modern performance. For the Greek audiences of this time were not spectators but participants in a shared communion. They were worshippers that had come to this festival specifically to take part in the ritual enactment of the death and resurrection of Dionysus and, in this case, it might even be claimed that Aeschylus was congregating them in order to evoke the blessing of the dead Agamemnon upon their own actions by means of ancient mimetic dances with which their ancestors had celebrated the life and suffering of their dead heroes. It seems more than likely that the chorus could have aroused the audience in the same way as they stirred up the young protagonists into action, by means of prayer and sacrifice:

LEADER

And the ripping cries of triumph mine
to sing when the man is stabbed,
    the woman dies—
why hide what's deep inside me,
black wings beating, storming the spirit's prow—
    hurricane, slashing hatred! [195].

ELECTRA

Both fists at once
    come down, come down—
    Zeus, crush their skulls! Kill! kill!
Now give the land some faith, I beg you,
from these ancient wrongs bring forth our rights.
    Hear me, Earth, and all you lords of death [195].

ORESTES

Father, king, no royal death you died—
give me the power now to rule our house [198].

ORESTES

O Earth, bring father up to watch me fight [199].

It is believed that when the Theater of Dionysus was rebuilt in
stone in the fourth century it accommodated between 14,000 and
17,000 people. Even if there were considerably fewer in the fifth century
B.C., one can, perhaps, be justified in imagining several thousand spectators roused at this point to holy indignation.

Northrop Frye describes the tragic hero as one who becomes increasingly alienated from his community and his chorus, isolated in his
solitary heroic vision,[29] yet in Aeschylus' play we not only see the chorus
(which, after all, is the only society we have on stage) goad Orestes,
Electra and the audience alike into a veritable frenzy of revenge, but
we see them skillfully and deliberately veer the passionate youth from
idle talk into action:

LEADER

> And a fine thing it is to lengthen out the dirge;
> you adore a grave and fate they never mourned.
> But now for action—now you're set on action,
> put your stars to proof [200].

This tragic hero is acting on behalf of his community. He is performing
an act of enfranchisement for the thousands of Athenian males that are
congregated here.

The story of Orestes and Agamemnon is first recorded by Homer
in the third book of *The Odyssey*. Here morality or personal compunc-
tion are not at issue, but only the duty of a son to avenge his father:
"What a good thing it is that a son should be on the spot when a man
is dead." This is the early Homeric heroism that we see even more
clearly in the ego, warrior-oriented behavior of *The Iliad*. It is the Greek
arete: human excellence made manifest by means of a display of
courage, a defiance of death and danger for personal honor. It constitutes manly, heroic bearing and bears no relationship to morality or
ethical behavior. This is a far cry from the Aeschylean hero who is torn
between the masculine, duty-oriented threat of Apollo, and the
strangulating female hold of the Erinyes, embodiments of his personal
conscience.

The essential differences, then, between Aeschylus' play and its
Homeric source are two. For Homer, the fate of Clytemnestra is not
even worth mentioning. His emphasis is on the masculine and the

heroic, whereas Aeschylus' is on the human and the moral. Homer's hero "gave a funeral feast to the people over his hateful mother and Aegisthus* the coward"[30] to celebrate his victory over Aegisthus, whereas Aeschylus' Orestes is driven insane by the guilt of his matricide, as dramatized by the Erinyes, those hideous projections of the Athenian male's tie with and fear of the female. And secondly, in Homer there is no mention of Orestes' sister or female counterpart, yet Aeschylus' dramatic account of the emerging hero accords the most prominent position to the female figure of Electra.

Aristotle describes tragedy as a situation play, as the mimesis of action brought about by certain situations.[31] After the evocation of the paternal spirit, the action within *The Libation Bearers* becomes that of Orestes seeking entrance into the house of his mother. Orestes had been torn from his mother as an infant. It is his return to her, and the violence that ensues, a violence that is commensurate with the overwhelming emotions that he has harbored for his mother since his banishment and which he experiences now at the moment of his reunion with her, that constitutes the main action of this play. At the same time, it is his confrontation with and murder of his mother that constitute the hero's (and the growing adolescent's) passage to manhood.

In *The Rise of the Greeks* Michael Grant describes the precarious relationship that seems to have existed between the sexes in fifth-century Athens. "Of course," he says:

> . . . family affection existed, as anywhere (tombstones bear witness to such feelings), and it would be absurd to deny that women were indispensable in all the obvious domestic ways.[32]

However, for an accurate account of those times, Grant relies on the writings of Hesiod and Semonides:

> A great amount of the literature of the Greeks echoes their poisonous hatred of women—or rather reflects a deeply anxious fear of them and of what they might be capable of doing. For in this repressively male-dominated society, marked by a voluminous sexual vocabulary and by exaggerated obscenity at festivals, there existed a curious sort of sexual *apartheid*. Despite their obvious indispensability for procreation, women seemed a mysterious, dangerous, polluting, "other" element, and the Greeks were acutely afraid that they might get out of step, might break out from their appointed and domesticated place.[33]

The spelling has been normalized as are all the names in this work.

In Euripides' play *Orestes*, the hero defends his act of matricide with
the following words:

ORESTES

In your defence, no less than in my father's cause,
I killed my mother. For if wives may kill husbands
And not be guilty, you had all best lose no time,
But die today, before your wives make slaves of you,
To vindicate her would be a preposterous act.
As things stand now, the traitress to my father's bed
Has paid for it with her life; but if you now kill me
The law is void; the sooner a man dies the better,
Since wives lack but encouragement, not, enterprise.[34]

Grant says that:

> ... religion was the one exception to the absence of women from
> Greek public activities. They were permitted their own rituals, such
> as the Thesmophoria, in which they played a leading and exclusive
> part (with outspoken stress on their role in fertility). For it was recog-
> nized that the deities had their wild, savage, untamable side — so
> sharply opposed to the orderly male culture of the "normal" Greek
> civilization — and that women seemed well suited to serve this aspect
> of the divine world, full of disruption and inversion, in which
> customary rules were in abeyance. After all, that was how Greeks
> thought of marriage; as the taming of wild, ungovernable, basically
> irrational womanhood. Thus many a Greek vase shows a man leading
> his wife off forcibly by the hand into her wedding, which amounted
> almost to a symbolic death.[35]

The misogyny of the young Hippolytus in Euripides' play of that name
is not necessarily an aberration:

HIPPOLYTUS

Zeus! Why did you let women settle in this world of light, a curse
and a snare to men? If you wished to propagate the human race you
should have arranged it without women. Men might have deposited
in your temples gold or iron or a weight of copper to purchase offspring, each to the value of the price he paid, and so lived in free
houses, relieved of womankind. Here is a proof that woman is a great
nuisance. The father who begot her and brought her up pays a great
dowry to get her out of his house and be rid of the plague. The man
who receives the poisonous weed into his home rejoices and adds
beautiful decorations to the useless ornament and tricks her out in
gowns — poor fool, frittering away the family property. (He is under
constraint: if his in-laws are good people he must keep his cheerless
bed; if his spouse is agreeable but her relatives useless, the evil he

must accept oppresses the good.) Happiest is he who has a cipher for a wife, a useless simpleton to sit at home. A clever woman I hate; may there never be in my house a woman more intellectual than a woman ought to be. Mischief is hatched by Cypris in clever women; the helpless kind is kept from misconduct by the shortness of her wit. No maids should be allowed near a wife; beasts that can bite but cannot talk should be their only company in the house, so that they could neither address anyone nor receive speech in return. As it is, the vile women weave their vile schemes with-in, and the maids carry word outdoors.[36]

Let us look at the way the women within this world regard romance:

CHORUS

Eros, Eros, ... may you never show yourself to me to my hurt, may you never come inordinately. Neither the flash of fire nor the bolt of the stars is more deadly than the shafts of Aphrodite which Eros, Zeus' boy, hurls from his hands. ... Eros, tyrant over men, chamberlain of the dearest bowers of Aphrodite, the destroyer that brings all manner of calamities on mortals when he attacks.[37]

Grant writes that "in most Greek city-states a woman had in law no standing in any question relating to her marriage, any more than she possessed other legal rights."[38]

In his book *The Glory of Hera* Philip E. Slater describes the extent of the segregation of the sexes within fifth-century Athens and the devastating effect that he believes this had upon the maturing male of that society.[39] He questions the pathological dependence that he believes Athenian males must have had upon their counterparts that could have provoked such an artificial separation. Classical Greece was essentially a male dominated society in which women were segregated within their own houses. Men came to their wives only in order to engender children, while for sexual and social pleasure they enjoyed the company of young boys or prostitutes.

In the Greek states men were obliged by law to marry—which is surely an indication of their reluctance to do so. Slater writes that "many Greek cities punished celibacy as a crime, and at one time Sparta denied the rights of citizenship to the man who did not marry."[40] It was rare that they married before the age of 30 or 35, the limit required by law, for they delayed the obligatory act as long as possible.

The wives they took were hardly women. Barely pubescent girls in their early teens, these brides would more often than not offer up their dolls to their family goddesses in exchange for their husbands, a less than fair trade. Girls were marriageable commodities to their fathers. They were forced to lead a stiflingly sheltered life before marriage, as their virginity was guarded by the father for economic reasons at all cost. Girls, of course, did not know their husbands prior to marriage and, for the most part, were married to men 15 to 20 years older than they. In marriage they left the loving care of their mothers and the familiarity of their homes and their family gods to live in the house of a total stranger. There are several accounts in Greek mythology of women that find and adopt abandoned babies, leading their husbands to believe that they are the natural fathers. Indeed, one version of the Oedipus myth also claims that Merope, or Periboea, told her husband Polybus the same story. Surely such a ruse can be feasible only where the husband is estranged from his wife.

Slater maintains that the reason for such segregation of the sexes is the innate fear that the Greek male had of the opposite sex. By virtue of their youth these brides bore more resemblance to young boys than to women. They were, for example, obliged to shave off their pubic hair before marriage, in order not to repulse their husbands. This fear of female sexuality on the part of the male can be traced back to a primal male fear of the *vagina dentata*, represented by the mythical Gorgon heads, gaping, tooth-filled female faces surrounded by snake-hair, most familiar to us perhaps in the image of the Medusa. It is significant, then, that the Medusa myth, which Freud interprets as an embodiment of the male fear of castration, the tooth-filled head being a threatening female sexual image and the snake hair, a deliberately misplaced image of pubic hair, is a projection of the Greek mind. Slater quotes Ferenczi as claiming that

> . . . in the analysis of dreams and fancies, I have come repeatedly upon the circumstance that the head of Medusa is the terrible symbol of the female genital region, the details of which are displaced "from below upwards." The many serpents which surround the head ought — in representation of the opposite — to signify the absence of a penis, and the phantom itself is the frightful impression made on the child by the penis-less (castrated) genital.

And he says that Bettleheim mentions

> . . . the frequency with which disturbed boys are concerned about the "hairy vagina," and suggests that it is "related to fear of the vagina dentata."[42]

Slater makes the claim that Orestes is very much a disturbed boy who has never been able to forgive his mother for having rejected him as an infant. He claims that the hero's boast when challenged by Menelaos in Euripedes' *Orestes* that he "can never have" his "fill of killing whores" is "a sentiment frequently expressed by sex-killers, and one which reveals again the importance of maternal seductiveness in generating pathology." Slater regards Orestes' act of matricide as an unsuccessful attempt on his part to rid himself, once and for all, of the excruciating need for maternal affection from which he has always suffered. He maintains that the fiendish presence of the Medusa-like Erinyes in *The Euminides* bears witness to the feelings of "longing and guilt" that his matricide had failed to assuage.[43] For Slater, the Erinyes are direct projections of the Athenian male's fear of female sexuality, much as witches were associated with women in the Middle Ages:

> ... during the persecutions which periodically convulsed Europe between the thirteenth and the seventeenth centuries, witches were often shaved in order to uncover the mark of the Devil.

It is of interest that Slater also quotes Semonides of Amorgos, who compared women to "sows, vixen, bitches, donkeys, weasels and monkeys,"[44] for it is surely no mere coincidence that all of those animals have themselves, over time, been described as the devil.

By virtue of her very existence, then, the Greek woman aggravated the male's already existing fear of castration. The demand, the neediness, the receptiveness of the woman's body and emotional state, combined with the seeming magic with which the woman engendered and nursed life, must have threatened the male with a sense of his own inadequacy, a fear of his own extinction. Masculinity was in danger of being devoured, consumed within the body of the female. From this it would seem that the ultimate male desire was to be totally independent of his female counterpart, a desire which is adequately demonstrated by the social independence of the male and by his predilection for those of his own sex. Unfortunately, the law of nature (as no less the law of the state) demanded communion with women. Myths such as the birth of Athena from the head of Zeus, supposedly without the help of the female, and the second birth of Dionysus from the thigh of Zeus, together with the all-male birth of Apollo, are surely projections of the Greek male's deepest need, a need to be totally self-sufficient.

The deserted girl-brides were left only with their children. Daughters were undervalued as were the mothers, so while the mother-daughter relationship might well have been a sympathetic one of a shared fate, the son absorbed the major focus of the mother's frustration. Slater maintains that the Greek mother used her son as "her little man,"[45] to fulfill her sexual and emotional needs, thereby terrifying the young boy with an overwhelming female sexuality which he could never hope to satisfy, a relationship which must have recreated on a personal level the collective male terror of the Medusa. Perhaps an idea of the son's sense of sexual inadequacy and his terror of rejection on the part of the mother is best reflected in the story of Hera, who engendered life and gave birth totally unaided to Hephaestus. Hephaestus was lame (which, in Freudian terms, would mean sexually impaired) and ugly. Consequently, Hera threw him out of heaven in disgust. Clytemnestra's murder of her husband and her extradition of her son accomplish not only Orestes' banishment from heaven, they also constitute a matriarchal rebellion, a total eradication of the masculine from her home. Moreover, the actions of this queen — on stage — manifest the Athenian male's worst nightmare.

In this context, the significance of the relative weakness of Aegisthus as a masculine figure, and his abstention, in terms of the myth, from the Trojan war, together with Orestes' own surprise when confronted with his mother's very real expression of love for Aegisthus, become clear. Clytemnestra sincerely mourns her paramour when he is murdered, for she has not regarded him as a masculine antagonist:

CLYTEMNESTRA

Gone, my violent one — Aegisthus, very dear.

ORESTES

You love your man? Then lie in the same grave [216].

Slater maintains that the mother was prone to torture her son as a representative of the male sex and as her husband's natural and political heir, so the Greek male, like Orestes, was often victim of a frustrated and hysterical woman. Also, the mother could use her son as a vehicle of her revenge upon her husband as we see Clytemnestra do with zest on Agamemnon's return from Troy:

CLYTEMNESTRA

Our child is gone, not standing by our side,
the bond of our dearest pledges, mine and yours;
by all rights our child should be here...
Orestes. You seem startled.
... Men, it is their nature,

trampling on the fighter once he's down.
Our child is gone. That is my self-defence
and it is true [136].

When we look at the creation myths of classical Greece, we see the
projected wishes and fears of the Greek male. Mythical women bear
little or no resemblance to the virginal child-brides that the Greeks
married. Neither do the Amazons of Greek theater. Rather, they seem
to be embodiments of the male's childhood fears of his mother. For the
most part, mythical women are full-blooded, highly-strung, tempestu-
ous and dangerous. Zeus roamed constantly in search of love-affairs as
did Theseus and the vast majority of Greek males, seeking (Carl Jung
would claim) to find their mother in woman after woman. Yet the king
of gods was ultimately cowed and answerable to the insatiable and
jealous Hera, and the great King Agamemnon returned victorious from
ten bloody years at war to be killed in his home by his queen. Could
it be from the mythical goddesses that Jung developed his notion of the
mother archetype—magnetic, demanding, devouring, life-engendering and murderous?

Gaea, or Ge, goddess of the earth, engenders and holds within her
belly all life; that is, she is the source both of life and of death. She is
the Greek male's idea of Woman, and Woman in turn is represented
in mythology by the equally paradoxical figure of the snake. In a phallic
sense, the snake obviously represents the male, yet, by means of the
snake's ability to devour animals in their entirety, at which time its
body bulges with life as does the body of the pregnant woman, it is a
representation of the life-engendering and life-devouring female. The
bringing together thus of male and female polarities within one symbol
in itself represents, it seems to me, an inability on behalf of the male
to separate himself from the female and to experience himself as an
autonomous being.

We must remember that a child's earliest state is one of total narcissism, one in which the child is aware only of its own needs. At this
stage the child is in a total symbiotic fusion with its mother. For both,
the oral satisfaction of the infant is the only priority. Thus, the mother
and child together form one being, one narcissistic entity. Slater presents a fascinating argument to the effect that

> ... the serpent represents the oral-narcissistic dilemma because it is
> the most common symbol of boundary-ambiguity. It appears in con-
> nection with the boundary between life and death, consciousness and
> unconsciousness male and female.... Thus the sexual organs receive

serpentine associations primarily because copulation blurs the
boundaries of the organism.

Does it not follow from this that copulation causes a recurrence of
man's earliest and happiest state of fusion with his mother? Slater
claims that "the snake represents the insatiable hunger of the child
itself—the desire to gobble up the mother and keep her forever inside."[46] Yet, for a man with as damaged a sense of self as the Greek
male, this blurring of the boundaries must have posed the ultimate
threat, the threat of a repeated and terrifying loss of his masculine
independence.

After having spent the first seven to eight years exclusively under
the manipulation of his mother, it seems more than possible that his
sudden wrench into an all-male world was accomplished before the
child had fully relinquished his narcissistic need of his mother. The intensity of the adult male's resistance to the female is surely commensurate with and indicative of the intensity with which his unconscious,
childhood self longed for total fusion with her.

What is it that propels *The Libation Bearers* into action? Surely it
is Clytemnestra's dream of the snake, a monster with which Orestes instinctively identifies. The queen dreams of the snake between night
and day, between a conscious and an unconscious state. It is a dream
in which she nurses her infant son, a fantasy world in which her deepest
wish and her most dreaded fear are realized: to be bonded with her
child. Only in dreams is the image of the snake so charged with significance. It is a dream that brings on the fear of the grave and of retribution and as such it lies in the dim region between life and death:

LEADER

She dreamed she bore a snake, . . .
. . . she swaddled it like a baby, laid it to rest.

ORESTES

And food, what did the little monster want?

LEADER

She gave it her breast to suck—she was dreaming.

ORESTES

And didn't it tear her nipple, the brute inhuman—

"She dreamed she bore a snake." *The Snake Goddess*, ca. 1600 B.C.E. Archaeological Museum, Heraklion, Crete, Greece. Photo: Giraudon/Art Resource, New York.

LEADER

Blood curdled the milk with each sharp tug . . .

ORESTES

No empty dream. The vision of a man.

LEADER

. . . and she woke with a scream, appalled,
and rows of torches, burning out of the blind dark,
flared across the halls to soothe the queen.
and then she sent the libations for the dead,
an easy cure she hopes will cut the pain. . . .

ORESTES

If the serpent came from the same place as I,
and slept in the bands that swaddled me, and its jaws
spread wide for the breast that nursed me into life
and clots stained the milk, mother's milk,
and she cried in fear and agony—so be it.
As she bred this sign, this violent prodigy
so she dies by violence. I turn serpent,
I kill her. So the vision says [201-2].

It is a Macbethian nightmare.

Slater makes the point that the failure of Orestes' matricide to cure
him of his maternal longings becomes apparent by means of his con-
tinuous dependence on women figures. He points out that ultimately
Apollo, the much flaunted patron of Orestes, fails to help him. Rather
it is Athena, combination of the male and the female, who restores the
balance of nature—Athena, whose Olympian virginity protects Orestes
from the threat of sexuality yet who, significantly enough, still carries
the sign of the snake over her robes, relic perhaps of her original
pre–Hellenic status.

Myth tells us that Gaea, earth mother, is born of chaos, that is,
that Chaos ruled before the Mother and that the Mother is a barrier between chaos and the child. It is the mother that prevents the child from
regressing to the point of what Freud considered humankind's instinctual desire for self-destruction. (It must again be stated that the
Western European creation myth, from earliest times to our own
post–Freudian period, has regarded the "child," "man" or "mankind,"
and the "hero" as male.)

The sedentary, nurturing aspect of the mother is evident in this neolithic sculpture from Malta, *Sleeping Goddess*. National Museum, La Valletta, Malta. Photo: Scale/Art Resource, New York.

It seems, then, that the object of primal man's fascination was the sedentary, nurturing aspect of the mother. The primal order was that of the nurturing female. She was the first order of human experience. We are told that Gaea gave birth to Uranus (sky) without a mate. Is this not another reflection of the male's fascination with the female's ability to give birth? Next we learn that Gaea marries her son Uranus and through him gives birth to the Titans, the Cyclopes and the Hundred-Handed, giants and monsters of the human psyche. Thus, the first scene of Greek creation demonstrates man's dependence on his mother and his desire through her to gain power and to engender the daemons which have throughout human history represented his innermost fears. By thus projecting his nightmares into monsters man could confront them and perhaps reach some measure of control. But it is the mother — primal, ultimate Woman — that is regarded in the male psyche as the source of such control and, as such, is the primary object of man's desires. According to Freud, all wives, all other female love-objects, are but displacements of man's primary need for his mother.

Uranus hid his children, the Cyclopes and the Hundred-Handed, within the body of Gaea, that is, within the earth, thereby "causing her great pain." "She resented this tyranny. Making a sickle of flint, she urged her sons to punish her father with it."⁴⁷ Do we not see in this masculine projection of intercourse a desire to destroy the female, together with the male sense of inadequacy in that he can only "inflict pain"? Simultaneously, we see both a fear of the newborn and a sense that the wife uses the fruit of her womb as a weapon against her husband, a weapon with which to replace his own time-limited power.

For we have three generations of male sky gods within the creation myth: Uranus, Chronus, and Zeus, and one life-engendering, life-devouring, castrating mother-goddess, Gaea. The sky gods, gods of light and of intellect, rise like men to their zenith at the midday of their lives, wane and are replaced by others; but Gaea and her daughters, the Erinyes (earlier, chthonic goddesses who, it is believed, were indigenous to these Greek isles before the Doric invasions, and were only later married into the Olympian system) are of the earth, self-engendering, self-perpetuating and, thereby, eternal. All of the three primary sky gods attempt to devour their male offspring. Uranus buries the Cyclopes and the Hundred-Handed within the body of Gaea (for which he is castrated by his son); Chronus is warned that his sons will overthrow him and therefore he devours them; and Zeus, warned by Gaea that his first wife Metis will bear him a son that will rule heaven, swallows his wife. Is it a coincidence that with a repetition to the amount of the magical folk-number three, the Greeks relived and reworked the fear of their own mortality and of life-engendering and therefore immortal woman to the point that they could establish a god, Zeus, who, though subject to the universal marital strife, was yet master of his universe? For it was surely only when he could establish male supremacy in the heavens, and rule by the power of the human spirit, that man could see himself as master of his earth.

I suggest then that the basic male anxiety played out within Greek mythology, was not caused primarily by his female counterpart, but was rather a reflection of his need to work out his own place within the universe. It represents a longing and an inability, on the part of the male, to accept his own mortality. Again we can be reminded of Aristotle's claim that meaning is conveyed by action. The action of Orestes reentering the palace of his mother and confronting her there encapsulates the ambivalence of the male creation myth. It represents both his longing to return home, and his need to separate the world parents—the earth from the sky. It personifies his human desire to regain the paradise of his earliest symbiotic tie with his mother, and his urge to overpower the fecund, repressive female. It enacts the ultimate male fantasy: to identify only with the masculine and, by so doing, to establish oneself as spiritual master of a male-dominated world.

As we have said, Homer's heroism had been a totally warrior-oriented, masculine concern, but for Aeschylus, the issue is more problematic. For him heroism and the mature man necessitated a fully integrated personality, the coming together of the Electra and the Orestes as one. Electra was not created as a woman but specifically as a dramatic figure, as the twin counterpart of the male, a necessary adjunct to an otherwise incomplete hero. Yet her name, *A-Lektra*, means the "unmated," her story is essentially that of a woman who has been separated and that lives forever, imprisoned and alone. Her character consists only in that of a woman longing for deliverance. In fact, characteristic of the claim Grant makes that religious ritual or, more specifically perhaps, the practice of religious mysticism, was the one area in which women played an equal role to that of men, Aeschylus brings Electra alive only at the moment of the evocation of her father's spirit. Only then is she at one with her brother. Only then is she recognized as a speaking, feeling being. She serves, in fact, as do the women of the chorus as priestess to the spirit of her father and as a medium for the initiation of her brother into manhood.

Rites of passage for neophytes on the brink of adulthood were common practice among the mystery cults of ancient Greece, among Orophic mysteries, mysteries of Eleusis, of Thrace, of Mithras, Attis, Adonis, Isis and even of Dionysus. Though many of the ceremonies of these rituals are lost to us, the idea of the initiation rites seems to have been the enactment of a symbolic death and rebirth, death to the secular life that the initiates had led up to that point, and rebirth to the sacred and the sexual of their adult life. In talking of the rites of passage and of ceremonies of death and rebirth, Arnold Van Gennep says:

> Since Attis dies and is reborn, it is thought that the rites of initiation also cause her future worshiper to die and be reborn: (1) through fasting he removes the profane impurity from his body; (2) he eats and drinks from the sacra (a drum and cymbal); (3) he goes down into a pit, and the blood of a sacrificed bull poured over him covers his entire body; then he comes out of the pit, bloody from head to foot; (4) during several days he is fed only milk, like a newborn child. . . . [T]he neophyte came out of the pit covered with blood like the newborn child emerging from its mother's body.[48]

We have described Orestes' premature banishment from his mother as a spiritual death; we have described Electra as one of a chorus of women priestesses going down to the burial mound of the dead Agamemnon and pouring wine (blood) into the grave; and we have suggested that Electra with her prayers walks in the very footsteps of her hitherto dead brother and conjures him back into life before the congregated audience, an audience that is well familiar with such ceremonies. As with the ancient Egyptian myth of Isis and Osiris, a myth that was still popular in fifth-century Greece, the hero is here brought back to life by the sister-lover. Everything indicates that *The Libation Bearers* is the play of the hero's initiation and that Aeschylus is deliberately building upon popular and powerful ritual as a basis for his theater.

In all the plays under discussion, Orestes returns from a symbolic death. At the burial mound of his father, center stage, the hero is brought face-to-face with the challenge of his identity.

II

Sophocles: *Electra* (409 B.C.)

If we are to understand early Greek theater in the way that it has been presented so far, we will no doubt find that the form and purpose of theatrical performances changed drastically in the fifty years or so that are believed to have elapsed between Aeschylus' presentation of *The Oresteia* and the performance of Sophocles' *Electra*. In the latter play the burial ground has been removed from the central position on stage. Chrysothemis rushes to her sister from some other space to tell her what she has found on her father's grave. Instead of the burial mound, the statue of Apollo, masculine god of light and reason, stands at the center of our attention. It is to him that Clytemnestra offers her sacrifice and her self-serving prayer:

CLYTEMNESTRA

I speak as I must; hear Thou as I would be heard.
O Lord Lycean,
If it was for my good,
That dream of double-meaning that I saw this night
Let its fulfilment come; but if for ill,
Then let it fall on those that wish me ill.
If there be any plotting in secret
Against my present welfare, hinder them;
And grant that I may long live safe from harm,
Queen of this house and country,
Living in happiness with those who love me,
As I live now...
. . . .
Lycean Apollo, graciously hear me,
And grant to us all our desires.
The rest Thou surely knowest, though I be silent, . . .[49]

H. D. F. Kitto directs our attention to Sophocles' obvious use of irony in bringing the tutor on stage, immediately after this offering, with the false news of Orestes' death. The death of Orestes seems to be an answer to the queen's supplication. The deception inherent in this news stands in direct correlation to the corruption of Clytemnestra's prayer. Aeschylus' Electra had descended to the spirit of her dead father and there had conjured up Orestes, a hero, to avenge the wrong perpetrated against her household. In Sophocles' *Electra*, in sharp contrast to the primitive purity of the earlier play, Clytemnestra offers a hollow prayer, much like that uttered over two thousand years later in a similar situation by Shakespeare's Claudius, and receives an immediate, dramatic — and false — response.

The onus, in this work, is obviously on the human players rather than on the gods. The gravesite as sanctuary and as a medium for the balance of nature has been replaced by the statue of a rational and cunning god who is not unlike the Orestes of this play. Like the hero the god is scheming and guarded, yet, in some unfathomable way, he remains the avenging arm of justice.

The action in Aeschylus' *The Libation Bearers* revolves around Orestes, the hero who emerges from the obscurity of the preheroic state. It had been suggested in the previous chapter that Electra, as the dramatic image of the preheroic state, becomes Orestes. In Sophocles' *Electra*, on the other hand, the avenging hero seems to be split into two parts: the feminine and the masculine. Orestes murders within while Electra goads him into action, without. Sophocles' Electra represents the agons, the conflicts and sufferings of an older order, while Orestes and his tutor act in what Thomas Woodard, in an essay on "The Electra of Sophocles," calls "high melodrama": They are taciturn, purposeful, noble, successful, action — and goal — oriented. As such, they represent idealized Athenian masculinity.[50]

Electra is the victim of the actions of others. She comes out of the interior of the palace depressed, disheveled, dressed as a slave. Woodard maintains that she represents the interior of the woman's house which is present as a backdrop throughout the action and which serves as a permanent reminder both of Electra's royalty and of her degradation.

Woodard claims that despite her efforts to goad Chrysothemis into action Electra herself remains all talk, all tears. For most of the action she stands center stage, a dramatic embodiment of suffering for her father's memory and a stark, theatrical contrast to the unobtrusive but determined manner of Orestes and his companions. Orestes' attitude is pragmatic. He is practical. His stance is essentially untheatrical. Perhaps it is for this reason that many interpreters translate the original Greek poetry of his speech into prose:

ORESTES

I am trying to find the place where Aegisthus lives. . . . Which of you,
I wonder, would be so good as to tell them within that a long expected visitor is here? [Watling, 102].

Electra's attitude and speech, on the other hand, is lyrical and poetic:

ELECTRA

I know,
How well I know,
Through every month of the year
My river of life
Is a spate of sorrow [Watling, 94].

The theme of the play without Electra is that of revenge. Orestes
and his companions set a plot and carry it through with skill and cunning. Orestes is the personification of the Greek term *dolos*, a deceitful
means to a just end. His behavior is directed by erga—facts, actions,
things, but his actions are drowned by the mourning lyricism and emo-
tionalism of Electra.

ELECTRA

O the sad day!—Is this the confirmation of the news
that we have just heard?
. . .
His dust lies there. . . Please give it to me sir.
I want to hold it in my hands, and weep,
Weep over this dust, and remember with tears
All my sorrow and the sorrow of all my house
                    [Watling, 102–3].

Woodard maintains that Electra represents *logos*, conviction, imagination, inwardness. She is *physis*. She has the repetitiveness of nature.
She has nature's faithful adherence to blood ties and nature's inability
to accept compromise. Woodard claims that Electra's truth, like that of
nature, goes beyond appearances, beyond the surface truth or *erga* ap-
prehended by the senses or sensible intelligence.

In this play the female figure of Electra no longer represents the
premature state of the masculine hero. Orestes and his tutor open the
action with their cunning plan of action, but remain silent and unseen
after the matricide. Electra, on the other hand, languishes in despair
and spiritual death at the opening of the play:

ELECTRA

Alas, Alas!
. . .
Sweet light, clean air,
As wide as earth!
Each night that dies with dawn
I bring my sad songs here
And tear my breast until it bleeds [Watling, 71].

Yet at the end she looms larger than life, seething with vigor over the death and demise of her mother. The images she uses are images of death and, indeed, as a dramatic character Electra here belongs to the principle of death.

Electra is not as symbiotically close to her brother in this play as in the play by Aeschylus, though at the moment of recognition the two are drawn together into a close emotional bond. It is part of Orestes' scheme (*dolos*) to bring on stage the urn of his own purported ashes. With overwhelming grief Electra embraces the urn, ashes of her brother, and for that one moment, for the enactment of the deepest form of human pain, the urn assumes, on stage, the prominence of a dramatic character. More significantly, for that moment of mourning, the urn assumes the stature of the central burial mound that we had noted in Aeschylus' *The Libation Bearers*. As such the urn is a theatrical device that has grown out of the sacrificial altar, and even beyond, out of the center of death and fertility of the great mother.

As the embodiment of *physis*, nature, Electra clutches the ashes to her in an attempt to draw death into herself:

ELECTRA

You were never your mother's, always mine,
Of all in the house I alone was your nurse,
. . .
I dead in you, you vanished into death,
. . . .
. . . a—aa—a pitiful body a—a a—a!
You came a hard road, my love, it was my death;
A hard road, my love, my brother.
And now you must receive me under your roof
[Force, 79–80].

Electra had nursed her brother in time of death, and in death she now draws him to her. In these words we recognize the regressive pull of the earth mother.

Overwhelmed by Electra's grief Orestes reveals his true identity:

ORESTES

A-a a-a! What to say? Among the helpless words,
Which to choose? But I can no longer keep from words
[Force, 80].

Woodard claims that Orestes here steps beyond his *erga* and
reaches out to the *logos*, the *physis* of his earth-bound sister. She in
turn is so moved by Orestes that she transcends her own nature and
adopts his active ideology.

Thus, in an amazingly modern sense, Orestes and Electra represent two opposing sides of one personality: Orestes, the rational,
political man of action and of cunning so admired by the Greeks, and
Electra, the emotional, lyrical, more primal, instinctual and volatile
female so threatening to the Greek male.

Electra does not vanish from view at the point of murder as does
Aeschylus' heroine; rather here, the son murders out of sight while the
daughter rages on stage, goading her brother into action. Clytemnestra, Electra's mother, cries for mercy from within the palace, "Child,
child, pity your mother!" and Electra rails in full view of her audience:
"But you did not pity him, nor pity his father," and to Orestes: "Strike,
if you can, again" (Force, 85-6). After the murder of her mother, to
complete the action, Electra orders Aegisthus "Go in at once. The
struggle is not in words,/ But for your life" (Force, 88).

The heroic action of Orestes has liberated Electra from her
regressive, repetitive, earthly nature to the action oriented nature of the
sister-helpmeet. Death and the central burial-mound that we had seen
in Aeschylus' *Libation Bearers*, symbolized a moment ago on center-
stage by the urn of Orestes, has here been transformed into the theme
of the death and resurrection, the revitalization and the power of Electra herself. We are again witnessing the ancient theme, noted in the
previous chapter, of the mythic, dark, chthonic vortex of death and
rebirth, yet this time it is not the death and rebirth of the hero, but
of Electra, the imprisoned sister-helpmeet. What we need to examine
now is the nature of Electra's newfound power. What is the dramatic
purpose of the Heroine's rebirth? What is the nature of the heroine?
What is Sophocles' dramatic intention in ending his play with Orestes,
the murderer, off stage, silent and unseen, and with Electra ranting
savagely over the corpse of her murdered mother? Orestes' absence and
return at the start of the play still represent, no doubt, the separation

of the adolescent from maternal society and his return and rebirth as
hero, yet what kind of hero does he become at the end of this tragedy?
We have seen him here represented as the idealized Hellenic male, as
a man of *arete*, of heroic action, of skill and craftiness who, like the
heroes of Homer's *Iliad*, is intrepid and unflinching in his desire for
revenge and the restitution of family honor. If this is the case, why does
he not appear to us at the end of the action, crowned with the laurel
of victory?

In a sense we have no denouement, for we are given neither pangs
of remorse on the part of the murderers nor any sense from the protagonists themselves that the fallen house of Atreus has been reestab-
lished, only the silence of Orestes and the savagery of Electra. Order
might have been restored as far as the community (the chorus) is con-
cerned, but what has happened to the agents of that order? Matricide,
the most horrible of deeds, has been perpetrated and the play ends with
the chilling sight of Electra, unlyrical and unloving, metamorphosed,
in fact, more into the murderous figure of her mother than into any
image of liberation, looming large at center stage over the blood-
drenched corpse of Clytemnestra as the chorus chants and perhaps
dances a paean of liberation:

CHORUS

Now for the House of Atreus
Freedom is won
From all her suffering,
And this day's work well done [Watling, 117].

Again vengeance has risen out of death and despair, bringing in
its wake justice against the living. Sophocles' theater has made it painfully and dramatically clear that those who suffer from such an act of
retribution are not the victims, but the victors who remain with the
sword and the blood on their hand. As for the spectators, they must
be so horrified at the spectacle that they are jolted into their own private
and perhaps separate reexaminations of the entire issue of vengeance
and justice, for they have been confronted head on with the enormity
of the issue and the moral and psychological price that it exacts. Thus,
for the first time, Sophocles separates justice from morality. For a moment, the two opposing elements, the male and the female, have fused
for action only to fall forever apart, in the most Macbethian of manners,
after their horrendous deed. This is no Aeschylean ritual by means
of which the community of spectators are eventually purged of all

contradictions. Here, for the first time, the spectators leave the theater at odds with the characters and the action that they have just witnessed. It is this contradiction that forces audiences to assess the real purpose of the playwright, and to recognize that in theater the playwright might well be at odds with the action that he or she brings to life on stage.

Another theatrical theme that begins to emerge in Sophocles' *Electra* and which we will see later in a much more developed form in the theater of Euripedes is that in which sanity is represented as the voice of the political establishment (the Sophoclean hero is the projection of the Athenian ideal) and madness is represented as the irrepressible expression of the individual conscience, a moral, essentially female voice that is ultimately independent of and even dangerous to publicly sanctioned law and order. In describing the Greek peoples, H. D. F. Kitto writes:

> As Attic sculpture and architecture combined Dorian austerity with Ionian grace, . . . so for a short time Athenian life was able to combine Ionian liberty and individual brilliance with a Dorian sense of discipline and cohesion.[51]

But not for long, the Greek male's fear of his own nature made it necessary that he separate order from chaos, reason from instinct, impulse and appetite.

By means of these dialectics, Sophocles' art has moved completely from ritual to theater and, as theater, it has become not the centering, religious, ritualistic experience of Aeschylus but rather its opposite for it brings to life on stage the destructive rift within the soul of the Western human being. It has become the dramatic record of people as decentered, fragmented beings. In my view, Western theater from this point on becomes a quest for wholeness, an attempt to regain the psychological integrity that had been reached and maintained earlier by means of religious ritual.

As we have seen, the traditional hero is masculine because he is the projection of an all-male fear and an all-male hunger. Perhaps with time, as we move toward a more heterogeneous society, we will be able to reunite the divorced parities of the human being—the male and the female, the passionate and the rational. In a society which recognizes the essential interdependence of the male and the female within each individual we might see the hero change, we might mitigate his need for violence and revolution, or—who knows—we might be witness to the total disappearance of the hero.

Until that time, only the strident, hysterical, female voice of Electra calling on her brother to strike again, to kill their mother without mercy, together with the unspeakable horror of her subsequent silence, is left to reverberate in the minds of the spectators as they leave the theatrical arena, and the "hero" remains speechless throughout his act of vengeance. For him, as Jan Kott points out, as for Hamlet so many centuries later, the unfathomably painful "silence" of human experience "is all."[52] Until then, the dramatic figure and the human "hero" are as fixed as a Pirandellian character, condemned to play and replay for all eternity their dramatic roles, to question for all time notions of revenge, Jihad (holy war), an eye for an eye, loyalty, personal humanity and morality.

Orestes has emerged as the archetypal hero, as the challenger of the morals of an earlier generation and the herald of those of the next. He embodies the theatrical "raising of issues" which Herbert Blau suggests is the essence of theater, for he is the son coming into maturity, into his own vision of life, at the moment of his confrontation with the death of his father, and he comes equipped, each time, with the challenge of a new and unwanted moral perspective:

> Side by side in history with the idea of progress is a natural instinct for thinking of advance as an act of recovery. Our most telling compulsion is a loss. . . . It's also what moves us in theater.[53]

III

Euripides: *Electra* (ca. 400 B.C.)

Although Euripides was a somewhat younger contemporary of Sophocles, there is a radical difference between the elder poet's treatment of the Electra myth and that of Euripides. The sense of royalty, of ritual and of the avenging dead are removed from the latter. Here we have neither palace, altar, nor tomb anywhere on stage, only the humble shack of a peasant, for the subject of this play is not the aristocracy but the poverty of society and of the spirit.

The play opens with the traditional prologue as introduction to the action, but it is given by a tattered peasant, owner of this shack, whom the audience of fifth-century Athens, no doubt much to its shock, soon learns is the husband of the princess Electra. For the first time in Western tragedy aristocracy is wedded to poverty and the peasant assumes a personality far more stable and honorable than that of the fallen aristocrat: Though humble, this man is generous, level-headed and loyal. He has natural dignity and compassion. It is this dramatic innovation that forces the audience to question their claim and that of their society to nobility. Indeed, it forces them to question the nature of nobility itself.

Euripides makes other innovations to the traditional myth, for here Aegisthus is aggressively dominant over Clytemnestra. For his own safety he has put a price on Orestes' head and has married Electra into penury. For her part, Clytemnestra is a more human, a more fully developed version of her Sophoclean counterpart for she is perpetually tormented by her memory of Agamemnon's sacrifice of Iphigenia.

CLYTEMNESTRA

My father Tyndareus gave me to your father's care,
Not to kill me, not to kill what I love and loved.
And yet he tempted my daughter, slyly whispering
Of marriage with Achilles, took her from home to Aulis
Where the ships were stuck, stretched her high above the fire
And, like pale field grass, slashed Iphigenia's throat.[54]

G. M. A. Grube, in his essay on *Electra*, claims that though Electra does appreciate her husband's gentleness and the honorable way in which he has respected her superior status, she is so obsessed by self-pity and by her desire for revenge that she turns every facet of her life, even something as insignificant as drawing water from the nearby spring, into the issue of Aegisthus, Clytemnestra, and the wrongs that they have perpetrated against her.[55]

Electra is portrayed with skillful, psychological insight. Her mother has spent her life mourning Iphigenia, to the total rejection of herself; consequently, the venom of the daughter is directed squarely against the mother. Grube points out that Electra considers Clytemnestra the murderess of her father and Aegisthus merely her helpmeet, while, for Orestes, Aegisthus is the villain and Clytemnestra an added horror that is too awful for him even to contemplate. It is for this reason that we see Orestes hesitate before he mentions her: "the condition to which / Aegisthus has reduced me, murdering my father — / He, and my fiendish-hearted mother" (96). In fact, it is made quite plain in this version of the myth, in contrast to those of Sophocles and Aeschylus, not only that Aegisthus and Clytemnestra were equal partners in crime but that Clytemnestra's paramour has since that time assumed the position of dominant, repressive, masculine authority and has taken full command over her and her entire household, while she herself has been reduced to a pathetic picture of uncertainty and remorse.

Euripides skillfully leads his audience to the source of its social and moral sickness, for he presents the female on stage in her most neurotic and impoverished state as the dramatic personification of the deepest and most repressed fears of the Athenian male. In this way again, theater has become the physical embodiment of underlying social and psychological problems. Electra is neurotic, unbalanced and self-pitying. She exaggerates her position and revels in her poverty and her troubles. She has the arrested development of one who has been trapped in a cataclysmic disaster. Her husband begs her not to draw water from the well but she insists. Yet later she tells the guest, whom she does not recognize as her own brother, that she is forced to draw water. In like manner she refuses to accompany the chorus of supportive young women to the festival of Hera because she prefers to cling to her misery, yet later she tells the stranger that she is barred from any revels or festivities. Grube claims that the reasons Electra gives for wanting to murder her mother and the order in which she gives them betray her self-interest and her confused sense of priorities, for first she complains about her own misery, then she compares her wretchedness with the wealth and glory of her mother and only finally does she mention the desecrated state of her father's grave.

Orestes sees the unsuspecting Electra returning from the spring and hears her lament loud about her parentage and her stolen heritage. Apart from the obvious dramatic convenience of this scene in terms of its providing information for Orestes, it also reveals the perverse, self-interested nature of the heroine. Grube also draws our attention to the fact that when Electra first senses the presence of the strangers, she is thrown into a complete frenzy of fear, hysterically calling to the chorus to run for their lives though there does not seem to be any other indication of danger, and the other women on stage show no sign of fear. Later, after the murder of Aegisthus, without listening to reason, Electra is again seized by panic, this time almost to the point of suicide. This protagonist is unreliable and emotionally unbalanced. When asked by the stranger what Orestes should do, Electra reveals herself as a veritable virago, eager and ready to murder her mother:

ELECTRA

When I have shed
Her blood to requite his, then I shall die content [102].

Euripides' play is a starkly realistic portrayal of a loveless and deranged woman. She is manic, fiendish, yet pathetic in her manipulation of Orestes and Clytemnestra. To her the fact that her mother had saved her life by persuading Aegisthus to marry her to a peasant has no significance. Similarly, though she knows that Clytemnestra cares enough to come to her should she give birth, she cruelly toys with her mother's efforts to make peace, sadistically luring her into her hut for the final sacrifice.

ELECTRA

Please come in
To our poor house. Take care this smokey wall does not
Dirty your dress. Now you shall offer to the gods
The sacrifice that is due[56]

Hungry for vengeance till the last, this Electra directs her brother's reluctant sword and drives it home.

Euripides' protagonist is a far cry from that of Aeschylus or Sophocles. She is no longer the fledgling hero, nor is she the female spirit of remembrance. Rather, she is the tortured, twisted, misshapen image of a female principle that has been repressed into the image of death and destruction. Hers is the total insanity of one whose being is given over entirely to vengeance. Only the extreme act of violence can exorcise the hatred by which she is possessed. And indeed, after the murder, we see that Electra's venom is abated:

ELECTRA

Tears, my brother—let tears be endless.
I am guilty.
I was burning with desperate rage against her [126].

Do the purging and the tears bring the promise of new life, or do they emphasize the pathos of this now wasted shell of humanity? The end of tragedy is independent of happiness or sadness; it consists, as Northrop Frye maintains, in the correction of an imbalance of nature:

CHORUS

Your mind has returned to itself.
And blows now with the wind of truth [126].

Only now, too late, is the protagonist released from the stranglehold of hatred, able to appreciate what life and normal living have to offer:

ELECTRA

Oh what shall I do?
Where shall I go?
What happy company will welcome me
To a dance or a wedding? [126].

The denouement of this play brings us back to the words of Joseph Campbell when he talks of the nature of myth and of the way in which people cling to them:

preferring even to make life a hell for themselves and their neighbors, in the name of some violent god, to accepting gracefully the bounty the world affords?[57]

Matricide has brought about recognition and reversal. Orestes says:

ORESTES

Oh Phoebus, in the command of your oracle
Justice was hidden from me;
But in its fulfilment
You have made torment clear [126].

The gods are forces of irrational violence, and instruments of pain. Only through human suffering does the hero gain insight. Only after the violence can he gain a measure of wisdom. It is the will of the gods that is carried out in tragedy, not the well-being of mankind.

If it were not for the excessive repression of the more lyrical, spontaneous aspects within the soul of the Greek male of the classical period, a repression dramatized so explosively in Euripides' play *The Bacchae*, if it were not for those aspects, dramatically characterized as "female," there would, perhaps, have been little or no need for the violence which, in the final analysis, caused the downfall of the ancient Greek world. Female characters, in these plays, are dramatic representations of a flaw recognized by these playwrights, a flaw which was the direct result of an uncompromisingly male society.

The female spirit of survival, the need for revenge on the part of the rejected female world of fifth-century Athens, as represented by Electra, is the protagonist's *hamartia*. It is the violently repressed female that threatens the Greek male with destruction. The chorus which at the beginning had been so supportive of Electra now recognizes the enormous danger to society that she had epitomized:

CHORUS

Dear Electra, you did a dreadful wrong to your brother,
Forcing him against his will [216–7].

As for the Euripidean hero, the act of matricide has propelled him into an altered state of consciousness. For the dawn of civilization, as for the individually maturing adolescent, the destruction of the maternal represents the beginning of reality, the birth of tragic experience. Orestes says: "Avenging him I am pure; but killing her, condemned." The paradoxical nature of the human conscience, a conscience which experiences — simultaneously — two contradictory emotions, and which we see emerging for the first time in this play, is the nature of the modern hero. Furthermore, Orestes' action grants him awareness, awareness that he stands apart and essentially estranged from the world of matter by which he is surrounded — and that he is guilty.

What Euripides' theater brings home most forcefully is the change of heart that is experienced by the perpetrators of violence. It is as though the poet is trying to dramatize for his audience the aftermath of their wars and the mourning that they will have to undergo. His play ends with the keening of both protagonists and chorus crying over their wasted life and denied humanity:

CHORUS

Wretched miserable woman! How could you bear
To see with your own eyes
Your mother gasping out her life?

ORESTES

I held my cloak over my eyes, while with my sword I performed
sacrifice, driving the blade into my mother's throat.

ELECTRA

And I urged you on,
and held the sword, my hand beside yours.

CHORUS

Could any act be more dreadful? [127].

The gentle hero Orestes, forced against his natural inclinations into the
most brutal form of murder is now exiled, separated from his newfound sister-partner:

ORESTES

And now the love that I need from you
Is taken away.
I love you and you love me [130].

Like Cain in Genesis, the conscious, guilty hero is banished. Only
Pylades, his mute and constant companion, the shadow of his spirit and
his will, remains behind to marry Electra. Thus, in a supreme act of
poetic fantasy, the freed captive merges with the unexpressed loyalty
and love of the hero in such a way that his inner, spiritual life is fused
imaginatively and balanced with his earthly feminine counterpart. This
romantic union is, it seems to me, the vision that Euripides has for the
future of his city-states. It is what Jungians would call the *hieros gamos*,
the sacred marriage of opposites, the one union that is guaranteed to
produce perfect offspring. To the modern audience it is reminiscent of
Faust's or even Goethe's own imaginative evocation of Helen and Paris
as the perfect union and as representative of the highest feats of
Goethe's poetic creativity. Yet the Romantic poet could not maintain
an image of such perfection. It was the male flaw, the grasping intru-
sion of his own ego, that dashed to the ground the promise of such an
idyll. Euripides does not intrude onto his vision. He merely proposes

it as a utopian cure for the ills of his generation while maintaining throughout a clear-eyed assessment of reality.

Euripides: *Orestes* (408 B.C.)

In Aeschylus' play, the mound of the dead hero had been center-stage, altar-like, at the center of the action. Here, as in Euripides' *Electra*, the gravesite is conspicuously absent, for the central point of focus is not the spirit of the dead hero but the suffering of man. In this play, the Orestean figure is essentially moral man, one that is torn by conflicting ideologies, by irreconcilable moral codes: by the discrepancy between the personal and the public good and by his loyalties to both the male and the female within the social structure. Here he has the full support of the loving sister-helpmeet, yet, ultimately, the action is his. It is he that is a victim of the gods:

ORESTES

... You, I know, consented
In word, but it was I who shed our mother's blood.
I blame Apollo; he urged me to this hideous act,
Encouraged me with promises—and did nothing.
I believe my father, had I asked him face to face
Whether I ought to kill her, would have gripped my hand
And begged, implored me not to lift a sword against
My mother, since that could not bring him back to life,
While it doomed me to the agonies I now endure.[58]

The Euripidean hero wishes to do the "right" thing but is misdirected by the gods, by forces propelled more by an amoral impulse akin to that of nature, than by any consideration for the human being. Experience drags the hero into disaster. Insight is not granted him until after the fact, until after his irrevocable act of violence.

ORESTES

The gods have not spared me; I sink in agonies.

MENELAOS

What agonies? What is the disease that ravages you?

ORESTES

Conscience. I recognize the horror of what I did [313].

The Euripidean hero learns his lesson too late. It will be interesting to compare this protagonist with that of Shakespeare when we reach the Jacobean period, for there we shall see that the progress made by the man of modern consciousness over his forebears lies in the fact that he is granted insight before the deed, is ravaged by pangs of conscience even as he first starts to contemplate the horrors he has to face:

GHOST

> But, howsoever thou pursuest this act,
> Taint not thy mind, nor let thy soul contrive
> Against thy mother aught. Leave her to heaven,
> And to those thorns that in her bosom lodge
> To prick and sting her.[59]

In this play the hero's feeble situation is dramatized by means of the sickbed of the protagonist, and in a manner not unlike Clov's stage position in Beckett's *Endgame*, the ailing Orestes is propped up at the center of his stage and his world:

ELECTRA

> There is no fate so terrifying to describe,
> No bodily pain or heaven-sent cruelty so sharp,
> Which human flesh may not be destined to endure [301].

If there is the suggestion of a panacea for human suffering, it is in humanism, in the role of the friend, and it is surely for this reason that Pylades here, for the first time, assumes an active, verbal part. If there is a character in this play of heroic stature, it is surely Pylades who lives and is willing to die for his friend. In contrast, Menelaos' treachery consists of his unwillingness to commit himself to a cause. As Orestes tells him:

ORESTES

> Friends who in times of trouble are no longer friends
> Mock the true force of friendship with an empty name [316].

The Greek city-states were famous for their self-government and for the lengthy legal debates in which all factions of society were encouraged to participate and in which all sides of an argument were granted equal exposure. Euripides seems to be deliberately manipulating both the Athenian passion for justice and its love of debate for his own dramatic purpose:

MESSENGER

Well now, I saw a stream
Of people going to take their seats on that hill, where,
They say, Danaus first called a council of citizens
When brought to trial by Aegyptus. So, seeing this crowd
I asked someone, "What news in Argos? What has put
The city of Danaus in this flutter? Is there a war?"
"Look," said he, "don't you see Orestes there, coming
To stand on trial for his life?"
 . . .
When the full roll of citizens was present, a herald
Stood up and said, "Who wishes to address the court,
To say whether or not Orestes ought to die
For matricide?" At this Talthybius rose, who was
Your father's colleague in the victory over Troy.
 . . .
Next there stood up a man with a mouth like a running
           spring, . . . an enrolled citizen, yet
No Argive;
 . . .
Another rose, and spoke against him. . .
 . . .
. . . His words seemed sensible
To honest judges; and there were no more speeches.
Then
Your brother rose. . .

"In your defence, no less than in my father's cause,
I killed my mother. For if wives may kill husbands
And not be guilty, you had all best lose no time,
But lie today, before your wives make slaves of you. . ."
                                          [331–3].

By now we are familiar with Orestes' misogynist argument, yet here it no longer represents the unanimous view of the people. Euripides is appealing to the reason-loving, democratic Athenian, for whom reality implies a great deal more complexity than the comfort of a narrow, bigoted perspective. The point of the play, it seems to me, is that there is no one argument, no right or wrong. Human experience is multifaceted and the social being is caught in a net of ambiguities. We are presented with the arguments of all the disputants because this play is a trial and the audience has become, defacto, both judge and jury.

In a similar manner, the characters of Euripides are neither innocent nor evil. Rather, they assume the contradictory perspectives of opposing ideologies. Thus the messenger of Orestes describes the following scene to Electra:

MESSENGER

Pylades and Orestes walking side by side,
Your brother's head bowed, his frame shattered by disease,
Pylades like a brother sharing all his pain,
Tending his sickness, guiding and supporting him [331].

while Helen's Phrygian slave describes the same two friends from a different perspective:

PHRYGIAN SLAVE

The twin Hellenic lions.
One was the son of the famous general;
the other was a bad-hearted man,
The son of Strophius,
A man like Odysseus, who deceive you and say nothing,
A bold fighter, loyal to his friends,
A shrewd soldier and a bloodthirsty monster.
Curse him for his smooth treachery —
He was up to no good! [349–50].

and Menelaos from yet another:

MENELAOS

They tell me frightful news of violence perpetrated
By those two savage animals — I won't call them men [355].

Heroism to one is treachery to another. From the point of view of Orestes, Helen's murder is justified:

PYLADES

. . . Helen's death
brings satisfaction to all Hellas — to everyone
Whose son, or father, she destroyed, and every wife
She made a widow [340].

while from the perspective of her husband and daughter, it is the most despicable of deeds. Given the contradictory but equally persuasive perspectives of both sides, our own views vacillate together with those of the chorus of women who are, at first, indoctrinated by the dominant male ideology:

CHORUS

The daughter of Tyndareos, who has disgraced her sex,
Deserves the loathing of women everywhere [341].

yet who are easily swayed by the horrifying report of the Phrygian slave:

CHORUS

What of the other Phrygians in the palace?
Could they not help? Where were they? [352].

No emotion is constant. The impressive, and no doubt authentic
display of honor that Orestes exhibits in the face of death:

ORESTES

Come, sister, let the manner of our dying show
That we are royal and worthy of Agamemnon's line.
I'll show all Argos what nobility is, driving
My sword home to the heart; with equal courage you
Must do the same. Be umpire of our rival deaths,
Pylades, and wrap our dead bodies decently;
And take us both and bury us in our father's grave.
Goodbye. I'm going now to do what must be done [337].

disintegrates all too soon into a mean-spirited cunning:

PYLADES

Let's kill Helen — and send Menelaos raving mad.

ORESTES

How can we do it? I'm ready, if the plan will work [339].

The manner in which these friends scheme the deception, capture
and murder of Helen and Hermione — both in this instant defenseless,
trusting women — is a far cry from the masculine cunning that had been
so idealized in Sophocles' play. Here nothing is absolute. The ideal
takes on different connotations in different circumstances while
heroism shifts into expediency.
    This play seems to be Euripides' reaction to a failed heroic world,
to a world in which civilization, torn between absolutes, between contradictory idealized behavior patterns, becomes self-destructive:

ORESTES

> . . . I know I'm a polluted man—
> I killed my mother. But that is not the sole truth.
> I avenged my father; and for that act I am pure [319].

The world of the Greek *arete* hero was one which believed in the
unflinching pursuit of absolutes: honor that must be avenged and
murder that must be punished. Yet, ironically, it was a world that
thrust the hero into a realm of experience that was totally alien to that
of the ideal, and bound him on a rack of moral ambivalence from which
there was no release. Aristotle condemned Euripides' *Orestes* for its lack
of heroic consistency and for its escapist, *deus ex machina* ending. Yet
it seems to me that this ending is a deliberate, ironic demonstration of
the poet's practical realism, of his belief that only the impossible intru-
sion of the gods into men's lives can mitigate the self-imposed polarities
of a failed heroic ideal.

As in Aeschylus' *Libation Bearers* the protagonists pray to the spirit
of their dead father before embarking upon their act of violence. Yet,
by means of the democratic judicial system which has characterized the
play so far, the audience in this latter play is separated from the emotional and moral stance of the characters. Is the grave of the father on
stage or are the actors calling into the questionably empty air? An altar
to the god is no doubt present on stage, but we have already pointed
out the possible ironic implications of Apollo's last-minute intervention. Unlike the earlier play, these characters undertake the ancient
liturgy without the undivided support of the community of spectators.
In fact, this supplication, together with Orestes' later attempted
murder of Helen and his attack upon Hermione, seems to be an indication of the moral depravity into which the hero's initial experience of
violence has plunged him. The prayer is frighteningly modern in its
manipulation of the gods, and of "the noble cause" for the justification
of violence:

ORESTES

> My father, dwelling in the shadowy halls of night,
> Your son Orestes calls on you. We need your help;
> Come now and save us! For your sake I am condemned
> Unjustly. Though my act was righteous, I am deserted
> By Menelaos; now I intend to take his wife
> And kill her. Be our helper in this enterprise!

ELECTRA

Father, your children call on you. If from your grave
You hear us, come! We die for our loyalty to you.
. . .

ORESTES

I killed my mother—

ELECTRA

Father, your children call on you. If from your grave
You hear us, come! We die for our loyalty to you.
. . .

ORESTES

I killed my mother—

ELECTRA

My hand too was on the sword.
. . .

ORESTES

For offerings, receive my tears—

ELECTRA

My cries of grief

PYLADES

Cease now; let's to the work at once. If prayers can thrust,
Like javelins, through the deep earth, Agamemnon hears.
—Grant, Zeus, our ancestor, and holy Justice, grant
To Orestes, and his sister, and to me, success! [343].

Throughout the act the opposing arguments of the play have
mounted to the point of extreme dramatic opposition: purity of action
versus purity of heart. Euripides utilizes the ancient tragic form of
stichomythia as a theatricalization of the dialectics of the honor system:

MENELAOS

You would perform the sacred cleansing—?

ORESTES

And why not?

MENELAOS

Sacrifice victims before battle?

ORESTES

And would *you*
Be worthier?

MENELAOS

Yes; my hands are clean.

ORESTES

Your heart's corrupt [357].

It is an opposition that counteracts, once and for all, the effectiveness
of community ritual.

In addition, Euripides manipulates the ritualistic form of stichomythia for his own highly realistic, dramatic purpose — to demonstrate
the mounting anxiety of Electra and her chorus of women at the
moment of murder:

ELECTRA

I am afraid that someone standing to watch the palace
Might discover this murder,
And make disaster even more disastrous.

SEMI-CHORUS I

Come on, let's be quick;
I'll go here and watch the highway,
Looking towards the sunrise.

SEMI-CHORUS II

And I'll watch westward along this path.

ELECTRA

Turn your eyes to this side and that.

SEMI-CHORUS I

We are looking from left to right,
Then behind us, as you ask.
. . .

SEMI-CHORUS II

Who is that on the road? Look hard; who is it?
Some countryman prowling round your palace.

ELECTRA

Friends, this will destroy us!
At any moment he will betray to our enemies

SEMI-CHORUS II

Don't be afraid; you were mistaken, the road is empty.

ELECTRA

What of your side? Is all safe still?
Give us a welcome report
If all's clear over there, facing the court-yard

SEMI-CHORUS I

All's clear on our side; keep a watch on yourself

ELECTRA

Wait, now — I am going to listen at the door.
You in the house there!
Why do you take so long? . . .

When will you blood the sacrifice?
— They aren't listening. O gods, what misery! [344].

It is a dramatic technique that is guaranteed to whip the audience into
a frenzy of anxiety.

Again, in this play, an imbalance has been caused in what should
be a natural harmony between the feminine and the masculine, for
the feminine life principle which we had recognized in Electra's nurturing of her brother has once again been sacrificed to the "masculine"
principle of violence and cunning. Thus, when she reveals her blood-
curdling scheme to Orestes and Pylades, Electra is greeted with the ac-
colade:

ORESTES

Oh, what a manly spirit and resolve shines out
From your weak woman's body! You deserve to live,
Not die! Pylades, this is the wife you'll die to lose,
Or live to win as a rich blessing on your house [342].

If it were not for the forced and artificial wedding of victim and
victimizer that takes place here under the unlikely instigation of the
gods, the lives of both Electra and Orestes would be irrevocably con-
secrated to death and destruction. The pathetic attempt of the protagonists to unite on the brink of their own deaths is their attempt to
simulate a wholeness of life which can only be attained through the
union of the feminine with the masculine, the union of the nurturing
and the loving, with action. Electra's infusion of love into Orestes robs
him of what he has identified as his "manly" capacity for violence:

ELECTRA

My dearest! Oh, my darling brother! How I love
To call you my own brother! Our two hearts are one.

ORESTES

Oh, you will melt my firmness. Yes, I must hold you
In my most loving arms—come! Why should I feel shame?
Body to body—thus, let us be close in love.
Say 'brother,' sister! These dear words can take the place
Of children, marriage—to console our misery.

ELECTRA

. . . I wish one sword might kill us, one
Memorial carved in cedar-wood receive us both.[60]

In the first chapter of this work, we had identified the bark of the
tree or the coffin as a prehistoric Egyptian symbol of death and rebirth.
By means of their union in death, these divided protagonists aspire to
rebirth as one integrated being. For only when the masculine and the
feminine principles are not divorced from each other by means of their
blind dedication to violence can they hope for normalcy. Only the
fusion of the masculine and the feminine can bring about the birth of
a nation dedicated to life.

IV

Shakespeare: *Hamlet* (1601)

It was suggested at the beginning of this study that the origins of the Electra myth lay in ancient fertility rites and in the symbolic expression of these rites within the murder of the male by the matriarch and the incorporation of his body into the mother earth for the purpose of fertility. It was suggested that in patriarchal hands the focus of the murder was transformed primarily into that of the female (mother) by the avenging male (son), itself the story of what many believe was a patriarchal takeover of earlier matriarchal, mystic religions. Finally the story became that of the repressed female (Electra) as emblem of the stifled emotional life of a people and its desperate attempt to be liberated and incorporated into some vision of the future. More than likely, both Sophocles and Euripides were warning their generations of the violence that would ensue as the result of the artificial separation of the male and female principles within the Athenian male.

Ancient Athens experienced enormous military, political and social expansion. It is believed that prior to the Dorian invasions the Ionian peoples had enjoyed an autochthonic identity; a sense of individual, rural freedom that found expression in its artistic forms and in mystical practice. Between the Mycenean and the Hellenic eras lie vast, unrecorded "dark" ages. Our history starts as Athens becomes the center of the maritime league of nations, the Hellenic ruler of the known world, and institutor of organized, national religion. It is a Greece within which Protagoras could proudly proclaim the human as the measure of all things, yet which still in many ways clung to old, half intuited, half forgotten superstitions and forms of mystical expression.

Though empire-building was antithetical to the Greek concept of self-government, by the fifth century Athens had become an empire in spirit, size and stature if not in political reality. Conquest, foreign rule, expansion and constant warfare forced the hitherto fiercely independent nation of soldier-statesmen to resort to the hiring of mercenary soldiers and paid officials. As Athenian power expanded it became more and more difficult for its citizen-statesmen to maintain a balance

Bartolommeo Ammannati, *Ceres* (or *The Earth*), fountain/sculpture, 1560. Bargello, Florence, Italy. Photo: Alinari/Art Resource, New York.

between the polarities of their existence: between urban and rural living, between political, military and social action and personal reflection, and between ambition and self-confidence on the one hand, and faith in supernatural forces on the other. Contradictions such as these, which lay at the very core of the Athenian personality, reflect those which (if historians are correct) existed between the more emotional, mystical and lyrical nature of the indigenous Ionians and the reason and order loving Hellenes. They are, indeed, the same polarities that we recognize in Greek theater within the figures of the male-female opposition. A necessary balance between the two had been essential for the spiritual and psychological well-being of the ancient Greeks but had disintegrated as they moved from a god-centered to a human-centered world.

Within a period of a hundred years, as evidenced by works such as Aeschylus' *Oresteia*, Sophocles' *Oedipus*, and Euripides' *Hippolytus*, Greece progressed from a rural people that had placed implicit trust in the supremacy and omnipotence of the gods to a nation of at least semi-urban humanists, sophisticates and philosophers who entertained grave doubts about the omniscience of their deities and even graver doubts about the nature, power and position of humans within their universe. It might be correct to assume that, by the end of the fifth century, foreign rule, expansion and constant wars had plunged the Athenian hero into a state of self-doubt, despair and existential confusion.

It might well be argued that to read Shakespeare's *Hamlet* (whose source can be traced to a thirteenth-century Latin history of the Danes) as a play that conforms to the deep-structure of the Electra myth is to invite endless such free associations. This might well be. Nevertheless, both the structure of this play and the sociological background which fostered it seem to have teased an Orestes/Electra constellation into theatrical reality.

L. C. Knight describes Renaissance society:

> Social organization was marked by three general characteristics; the close connection of the whole population to the soil, the large corporate or cooperative element in the life of the people; and the extent to which the whole structure rested upon custom, not upon either established law or written contract.[61]

He describes the Renaissance social structure as one of different self-supporting, self-sufficient village communities, which were ruled not by edict, but by social reciprocity and mutual caring. Knight claims, for example, that village guilds would care for the needs of those members who had fallen on hard times, that villagers would raise funds for burials, for the marriages of young girls or for their confinement into convents. The peasants, he maintains, had a reciprocal, universally accepted, stable and mutual, if grossly unbalanced, relationship with their feudal lords. Knight claims that citizens had not yet developed a sense of national concern, that attention was focused still on village and on small town life. This does not mean, of course, that life was idyllic. England was subject to bouts of plague, high infant mortality, feudal strife, superstition and religious persecutions. Despite these horrors, the peasants shared a common understanding of God and knew their place and purpose in their world.

Like Athens of the fifth century B.C., England enjoyed enormous prosperity, expansion and a booming trade during Elizabeth's reign. America was discovered and American gold was introduced into Europe. England plundered exotic riches—spices and jewels from the Indies and the Orient. Drake undertook his first expedition in 1573 and from it he brought back enough wealth that England was able to free herself from her many overseas creditors and invest as much as £42,000 in what was to become famous as the East Indies Company. With increased wealth came increased expansion and the need for further conquests and discoveries; with increased expansion, in turn, came increased spending. England was involved in more foreign wars during the reigns of Elizabeth and King James than at any previous time in her history, and, as she hired mercenary soldiers, she had an ever increasing need for funds. Money-lending syndicates emerged and were the cause of the first growth of capitalism in England. With wealth and prosperity came a new class of money-makers, a blurring of class distinctions and a sense of loss and social confusion on the part of the peasants and the aristocracy alike. With capitalism came gross materialism, questionable ethics, and subjective morality.

Like Greece at her height of power, Renaissance confidence was built upon the knowledge that "man" stood securely at the center of his universe (with woman at his side) and that the earth turned at the center of the cosmic hierarchy. Copernicus' contradiction shattered the very foundation of human faith and left people floundering in disorder. Within this confusion, Machiavelli also had a profoundly disturbing influence. Not only did he instantly propel humankind into the modern age with his objective, scientific approach to the field of politics, but, by separating one aspect of reality from the collective whole and subjecting it to its own, independent criteria and moral code, he demonstrated the subjectivity and the fragmentation of all knowledge. With his theory of political expediency, Machiavelli destroyed all sense of global harmony and objective meaning and demonstrated the lack of unity within human experience. Reality was suddenly fragmented into a myriad disparate areas of experience, each subject to its own questionable laws of morality.

No facet of reality was exempt from disintegration. Universal belief in the Church as guardian of the mysteries of Hell and Eternity and as the medium for the salvation of the soul was itself under attack by Martin Luther's theory of personal redemption. Morality, always an objective matter of Right and Wrong, was now reduced to a personal and invisible struggle within the privacy of each person's very questionable human soul. The subjection of religion to the political arena of the Reformation with its incumbent cruelties and persecutions and the need for the Roman Church to defend itself by means of the Council of Trent all combined to complete the disintegration of the Renaissance spirit.

As with Greek theater, the art of the late Elizabethan and the Jacobean periods reflects a restlessness of the human soul, a sense that the world and the individual are inextricably interwoven, and that the individual is constantly confronted by the oppositions within the human spirit. Protagonists of Shakespeare's "dark" plays—*Lear*, *Macbeth*, *Hamlet* and *Othello*—are filled with such opposition, with the conflict between their public and their private selves, with the need to satisfy their immediate desires and yet to transcend the smallness of their natures. As with the Greek playwrights, Shakespeare provided a mirror of people perpetually struggling against the dualities and complexities within their natures.

Like Classical Greece, England in the Renaissance and Jacobean periods was essentially a male-dominated society with relatively rigid ideas regarding the appropriate status and demeanor of women. Linda Woodbridge gives the following quotes together with her own commentary:

> [As a man should] showe a certein manlinesse full and steadye, so doeth it well in a woman to have a tendernes, soft and milde, with a kinde of womanlie sweetnes in everye gesture . . ., that in goyng, standinge and speakinge . . . may alwayes make her appeere a woman without anye liknes of man. It is not comlye for a woman to practise feates of armes, ridinge, playinge at tenise, wrastling, and manye other thynges that beelonge to men.

Yet, though men might want to keep their womenfolk gentle and soft-spoken, underlying many of the writings of the time was the fear that in reality their true nature was sexual, wild and untrammable:

> Emonge them of olde time the maner was that women wrastled naked with men, but we have lost this good custome.[62]

Of the author of this last quote, Woodbridge writes:

> Aretino is an early practitioner of a tactic familiar in our own day—
> the insinuation that women who interest themselves in masculine
> pursuits are mainly desirous of gang rape.

Men of the Elizabethan period seemed fairly confident that

> Generallye everye woman wisheth she were a man, by a certein provo-
> cation of nature, that teacheth her to wishe for her perfection.[63]

Yet there are also those that defended woman, believing that if she did
wish to be like a man, it was so

> . . . that shee might be free from the filthinesse whiche men did force
> her to . . . like as ye litle chicke being caught by the kyte, would wish
> with all his heart hee were a kite, and yet the kind of kites is not to
> be thought better then of the chicken.[64]

The following quotation from Tasso bears an uncanny resemblance to
the mysogenistic writings of the ancient Greeks:

> If thou marry one that is faire, she will grow to be common: If one
> that is fowle, she will waxe loathsome. If (she) should chaunce to be
> good . . . must I loose her. . . . If shee should be badde, I must beare
> with her perforce: . . . and if shee be faire, I must keep a watch and
> guard ouer her.[65]

and with the following quotation from Tasso we come full circle back
to the mentality of the Classical Athenian male and recognize that the
need of Renaissance man to confine his female counterpart to social
niceties is nothing but an expression of his overwhelming fear of female
otherness:

> an unworthy and contemptible thing is a woman . . . not framed for
> any other respect or use, then for a Receptacle of some of our Ex-
> crementall humors: standing vs in the same steed, as the Bladder, the
> Gaull, and such other vncleanly members of our bodie.

Woman, claims Tasso,

> . . . is under the moon's pernicious influence, as evidenced by
> disgusting physical attributes—menstruation, thick phlegm, "driul-
> ing spettle," "smoking vapors comming from the stomack."[66]

One of the characteristics of the art of this period, which resembles
that of Classical Greece, is the sense of enormous human vitality, of ex-
plosive passion, and human will so volatile, it threatens to burst

asunder the seams of reality. Thus, again, in a society in which women are lauded for their pliability, for their discretion, for their devotion to their husbands, their humility, their piety and their chastity, we have a theater of Amazons, of sexually rapacious women and of women as passionate, as strong and as centered as *The Duchess of Malfi*, who, in the midst of sexual and political perversion, violence and madness, staunchly clings to her sanity and sense of self; of women as ruthless and deceptive as Beatrice in Middleton's *The Changling*; as corruptible as Bianca, in Middleton's *Women Beware Women*; as ruthless as Vittoria, in Webster's *The White Devil*; and as sensuously gullible as Mistress Frankford in Thomas Heywood's *A Woman Killed with Kindness*.

With humanism and the disintegration of the Renaissance spirit, theater returns to the tragic form, for tragedy is the expression of a society that has lost its religious optimism, its belief that ultimately God will save. Madness, so common a feature in Jacobean tragedy as in the ancient Greek form, is the result of a failed idealism and it becomes the only vehicle of expression open to *Hamlet*.

The Greek Orestes is told by Apollo to avenge the murder of his father and, despite the torment that he later undergoes, he never has any reason to doubt the nature and authority of the god. The spirit of the Aeschylean father enters into the son, propelling him into the heroic and tragic action that fixes him for all time as a figurehead by which to measure revenge, honor, justice and public versus private conscience. But although Hamlet has no qualms about the absolute quality of evil and knows beyond all doubt that regicide and murder must be avenged, his god is silent and the ghost of his father is questionable. By the time of the well Christianized society of the seventeenth century, the good and evil forces that had together comprised the dual nature of the Greek gods have been split apart into God and the Devil and need to be assessed for their validity, while the Aeschylean ghost that had been given so prominent a place at center stage and that had been conjured up so deliberately and knowingly until it took possession of the prime mourner, forces itself only on to the outermost perimeter of the Shakespearean stage, in the "very witching time of night"[67] when the spirit of the unconscious and of human conscience pull at the inner recesses of the mind. It is much like the Orestean-serpent of Clytemnestra's dream, filled with ambiguity and with the ambivalence of the mother- or father-son relationship. It is as an unwanted thought surfacing in the corner of an "enlightened" mind and threatening it with total collapse.

Hamlet's ghost, then, is not only a phenomenon of the otherness of the spirit, but a materialization of that anxiety which has characterized modern man since that time.

HAMLET

> Be thou a spirit of health or goblin damned,
> Bring with thee airs from heaven or blasts from hell,
> Be thy intents wicked or charitable,
> Thou com'st in such a questionable shape [1.4.44–47]

The ghost appears on stage, shrouded in the mist of the confused and questioning mind.

Here there is no central burial mound, no circular arena. Actors and spectators are not possessed by their dead; they need, rather, to test them. There is a conspicuous absence of a mourning space and of ritual in the court of Claudius, the secular king. The ghost is always off-center, on the parapet of the castle or in the bedroom, forcing himself into the mind, into the world of dream or fantasy, because the spiritual and the abstract are not accorded space in this Jacobean society. The ghost is desired and pitied, and yet the source of the most profound fears. He has many of the dangerous complexities of the Greek god or ancestors, yet the seventeenth century mind has to assess it and define it rationally.

HAMLET

> *Let me not burst in ignorance*, but tell
> *Why* thy canonized bones, hearsed in death,
> Have burst their cerements, *why* the sepulchre
> Wherein we saw thee quietly interred
> Hath oped his ponderous and marble jaws
> To cast thee up again. *What may this mean*
> That thou, dead corse, again in complete steel,
> Revisits thus the glimpses of the moon,
> Making night hideous, and *we fools of nature*
> So horridly to shake our disposition
> *With thoughts beyond the reaches of our souls?*
> *Say why is this? wherefore? what should we do?*
>   [1.4.50–61; emphasis added].

The seventeenth century protagonist lacks the unquestioning faith necessary to accept the ghost as a source of strength and heroism. Ironically, the Greek Orestes who was able to conjure up the spirit of the dead so easily by means of ritual had no difficulty in recognizing the separateness of the gods and therefore the imperative and objective nature of their orders. Hamlet, however, is tormented by the doubts of his Judao-Christian dilemma, unable to distinguish whether his Ghost is a product of God, the Devil, or the daemons within his own mind:

HAMLET

I am myself indifferent honest, but yet I could accuse me of such things that it were better my mother had not borne me: I am very proud, revengeful, ambitious, with more offenses at my beck than I have thoughts to put them in, imagination to give them shape, or time to act them in. What should such fellows as I do crawling between earth and heaven? [3.1.132–139]

> Observe my uncle. If his occulted guilt
> Do not itself unkennel in one speech,
> It is a damned ghost that we have seen,
> And my imaginations are as foul
> As Vulcan's stithy . . . [3.2.81–85]

Here, the spirit of Hamlet's father is not the masculine, Apollonian voice of male retribution so necessary for the hierarchical order and well-being of the patriarchal state, but the spirit of the Orestean dilemma itself. The Homeric *arete* hero had avenged the wrongs perpetrated against him free from any moral compunctions, the moral world of the later Greek poets questioned and struggled with the paradox of heroic action versus individual conscience, but the humanist of the post–Judao-Christian tradition is rendered completely impotent, frozen in his or her tracks with the self-doubt and the confusion of Western culture. Hamlet is the Orestes that can foresee the moral implications and the psychological torment implicit within the act of revenge, before the crime is committed. Can he assume the leadership of his country without "tainting" his "mind," without becoming a Claudius with his court of flatterers? The Spirit of his father-king warns Hamlet to "revenge his foul and most unnatural murder":

GHOST

> But howsoever thou pursuest this act,
> Taint not thy mind, nor let thy soul contrive
> Against thy mother aught. Leave her to heaven,
> And to those thorns that in her bosom lodge
> To prick and sting her [1.5.91–95].

Hamlet's aim is to maintain a mind that is free of guilt and to inflict his mother, not with death, but with the daemons within her own conscience. The modern hero is only too aware that the worst punishment is not physical death but human awareness. This Jacobean Orestes does not want to restore the fallen house of his father on a political level; rather, he wants to cure its sickness of soul. The part of his mind that conforms to the military and action-oriented ideals of his society has been processed by his environment but the other—his inner, moral voice that is so basic to his nature—bids him restraint, watchfulness and instruction. Susan Letzler Cole points out that Hamlet's intention is not to act but to speak.[68] Unlike the Greek Orestes, this hero's weapon is not the axe, but the spoken word:

HAMLET

... Soft, now to my mother!
O heart, lose not thy nature; let not ever
The soul of Nero enter this firm bosom.
Let me be cruel, not unnatural;
I will speak daggers to her, but use none.
My tongue and soul in this be hypocrites:
How in my words somever she be shent,
To give them seals never, my soul, consent! [3.2.399–406]

and, in fact, his closet speech to his mother has, if only momentarily, the desired effect:

GERTRUDE

... O Hamlet, *speak* no more.
Thou turn'st mine eyes into my very soul,
And there I see such black and grained spots
As will not leave their tinct [3.4.99–102; emphasis added].

Hamlet's doubts about the nature of his universe and his questioning of the spirit pull the audience emotionally on to his stage. The anxieties that are embodied on stage are the unspoken fears of all present, but it is that shared skepticism that makes Hamlet and all the thinkers of his day antiheroes, fathers of the whole tribe of antiheroes that populate modern theater.

Peter Brook claims that

> All religions assert that the invisible is visible all the time. But here's the crunch. Religious teaching ... asserts that this visible-invisible cannot be seen automatically—it can only be seen given certain conditions. The conditions can relate to certain states or to a certain understanding. In any event, to comprehend the visibility of the invisible is a life's work. Holy art is an aid to this, and so we arrive at

a definition of a holy theater. A holy theater not only presents the invisible but also offers conditions that make its perception possible.[69]

Is it fair to claim that theater has assumed the place and function of ancient ritual? In a myopic, secular world such as that which characterized the late Elizabethan and the early Jacobean, did the theater of Shakespeare create the "holy"? Did it bring to life, on stage, the buried uncertainties and horrors, the invisible Titans and Cyclopes within the soul of the modern person?

The world of Claudius' court, albeit spiritually stifling, would be centered wereit not for Hamlet. As we have seen, Hamlet is the hero in the sense that he forces into the complacency of this secular world his own revolutionary moral stance together with the dramatic embodiment of a spirit that has to be reckoned with within the space of daily life. In his need for a space in which to mourn, he journeys outward to the realm of the spirit and returns to force that spirit onto the space of the court and the Jacobean stage. Whereas it was the priestesses, Electra and her chorus of slave women, that had conducted the Aeschylean hero and the community of spectators to the source of inspiration within the burial mound, here, in the predominantly male world of the Danish court, it is Hamlet, the male heir, who has been so rudely separated from his mother and from the object of his romantic affections, who functions as the priest for his own community of Elizabethan spectators. The Greek hero had evoked the spirit of his father in an accepted manner, as a member of a community. The hero of the modern world does so as a rebel, in the silence and loneliness of his memory. Yet Hamlet is still the shaman, the actor, the adolescent emerging into manhood, and the Orestean hero, for he does voyage imaginatively outward into a symbolic death and return to materialize the abstract on stage.

Hamlet's philosophical bent and training gives him an outlook completely foreign to that of the world around him. Claudius keeps an anxious eye on his nephew and stepson because he expects him—as no doubt do others within the Danish state—to react physically, if not militarily, to Claudius' usurpation of the throne. But Hamlet does not think in terms of material action. His aim is to regain supremacy by means of spiritual maturity. For this he needs, not merely to enter the palace of his mother as Sophocles' Orestes had done, but to reach and adopt as his own the royal spirit of his father-king. While making a different point, Letzler-Cole points out that

In his dialogue with his mother, Hamlet's very use of stichomythia, the ancient mode of communication between the living and the dead, reveals the degree to which he has usurped the role of his deceased father.

Letzler-Cole also writes:

The Ghost's final command is "Remember me," and Hamlet "remembers" his father by assuming an antic disposition. His immediate reaction to the Ghost's revelation of regicide, fratricide, and adultery has been thought puzzling, especially in its emphasis on memory rather than on revenge:

> O all you host of heaven! O earth! What else?
> And shall I couple hell? O fie! Hold, hold, my heart,
> And you, my sinews, grow not instant old,
> But bear me stiffly up. Remember thee?
> Yea, from the table of my memory
> I'll wipe away all trivial fond records,
> All saws of books, all forms, all pressures past
> That youth and observation copied there,
> And thy commandment all alone shall live
> Within the book and volume of my brain,
> Unmixed with baser matter. Yes, by heaven!
> O most pernicious woman!
> O villain, villain, smiling, damned villain!
>   Now to my word:
> It is "Adieu, adieu, remember me."
> I have sworn it. [1.5.99–119]

Hamlet is to make his liminal journey in his mind. The act of recollection is the act of allowing himself to become haunted by what he wishes to recollect. Dying to his former self, "all forms, all pressures past," Hamlet is taking on the disposition of the deceased with a vengeance.... In Claudius' court, memory is a kind of revenge. Hamlet's "antic disposition" will eventually turn the court into the mourners they refuse to be, will provoke the response that his father's dead body could not.[70]

Letzler-Cole maintains that "the experience of death, though it may be universal, is inevitably solitary."[71] Perhaps it is the discrepancy that exists between the sense of isolation experienced by the mourner and the public and ceremonial expression of that mourning that lies at the heart of the pathos of the Electra figure. Perhaps it is this discrepancy that is the reason for modern human's alienation from and ambivalence with ritual, and perhaps it is this that provides the starting point for all the plays that fall into the Oresteian pattern:

GERTRUDE

Though know'st 'tis *common*. All that lives must die,
Passing through nature to eternity.

HAMLET

Ay, madam, it is *common*.

GERTRUDE

. . . If it be,
Why seems it *so particular with thee?*

HAMLET

But I have within which passeth show —
These but the trappings and the suits of woe
[1.2.76–91; emphasis added].

The audience is asked to journey imaginatively from the general form of ritual, "the trappings and the suits of woe," to the particular and personal suffering of the protagonist.

Only when I lost my own father was I hit by what I now consider to be the full import of these lines. Of course "'tis common, all that lives must die." It is with such equanimity that we accept the passing of others. But when it is our own loved one, our own mourning, when the death is "particular" to ourselves, then, and only then are we catapulted into an experience of pain and loss that defies the boundaries which divide this world from the next. If we could but feel that anguish at the passing of the stranger and at the passing of the loved ones of the stranger, if the deaths of others could be experienced with that same "particular" feeling as the death of the personal and loved father, we would forbid the shedding of a single drop of human blood. Surely, if we could feel such pain for others, wars would be abolished. Is this not also the suggestion made by Lady Macbeth when she says, referring to the murder of Duncan, "Had he not resembled/ My father as he slept, I had done't?" (*Macbeth*: Act II, scene 2, lines 12–3).

The quest of the hero is the human being's struggle with his or her conscience, and the purpose of heroic theater is to embody that struggle in its most naked and aching form. Hence the perpetual struggle of the hero with death and the father. Letzler-Cole maintains that

> The central shareable experience of death is the enactment of mourn-
> ing. In suggesting that this profound communal experience resides

at the heart of tragedy, I am clearly drawing on the power of mourning as an archetype, even in cultures which, like our own, do not
encourage fully released expressions of grieving for the dead. As
Geoffrey Gorer has cautioned, "a society which denies mourning and
gives no ritual support to mourners is thereby producing maladaptive
and neurotic responses in a number of its citizens."[72]

Mourning for Hamlet constitutes insurrection, "a course/ Of im-
pious stubbornness [and . . .] unmanly grief" (1.2.99–100). His mask
of madness is a neurotic reaction, but within the context of this court
it is the only way he has of assuaging his feelings of sorrow and resent-
ment. Ophelia, imprisoned like Electra in a loveless, sexless, youthless
world in which she can neither woo nor mourn, is forced beyond neuro-
sis into the abyss of that madness which Hamlet merely assumes.

It might be fair to suggest that Ophelia drowns in, or because of,
an all-male world. Unlike the Sophoclean Electra who lived in an all-
women's house, whose very being as expressed through her language
was that of Physis, the undammable force of Nature, the essentially
female, lyrical power of the earth who burst the confines of her prison
with a velocity that can be measured only by the extent of her repression, Ophelia's delicate sensitivity is buffeted clumsily by the grasping
materialism of her father and her brother. As a theatrical figure she is
an extension of the Electra that had been rejected by her mother. The
Greek Electra had turned her back upon female sensuality as a characteristic of her hated mother. Jan Kott writes:

> Electra is a king's daughter, deprived of all the privileges of her birth
> and station. In Sophocles she has been made to remain a spinster. . . .
> Electra has been placed in an enforced situation, having to make the
> fundamental choice between total acceptance and total refusal; ac-
> ceptance of her fate, or refusal to accept it; acceptance of a world in
> which her mother has murdered her father, or rejection of that world
> with all the consequences of such a decision. In Electra's argument
> with her sister Chrysothemis, just as in Antigone's argument with her
> sister Ismene, all the great oppositions are presented: loyalty to the
> dead and loyalty to the living; revolt against authority and obedience
> to those in power; renunciation and compromise. Electra is asked to
> forget, but she is the one who remembers. Electra's memory is the
> presence of the past and the foretelling of vengeance.

"Loyalty to the dead," "revolt against authority," "renunciation," and,
above all, "memory" and "vengeance" are characteristics of the Electra
(and the Antigone) figure, because they have become mythically and
theatrically indistinguishable from the female principle. Talking of

both the Antigone and the Electra figures, Jan Kott claims that "those who rebel against authority, against kings, who oppose their loyalty to the dead to their duties to the living, who refuse to accept the world, are mad."[73]

In fact, madness in the context of our theater has become associated with all the above-mentioned characteristics of the "female" as with femininity itself. In the Christian world this female principle has become subsumed within the ego-restraint of the rational, morality-oriented male. The female "mad" principle separates Hamlet from his society and thrusts him back into the liminal regions of memory and the spirit of his beloved father, much as Orpheus, in that beautiful Greek legend, had managed to recapture the beloved essence of Euridice by means of the lyrical power of his muse, but "loyalty to the living," "obedience to those in power," "compromise," and "forgetfulness" are masculine attributes and it becomes essential for the hero to eradicate the female within him in order to buoy himself for action and for life.

In the Renaissance play, the ambivalent situation that Electra had entertained vis-à-vis those of her own sex is accelerated even further: not only does Ophelia have no mother to recognize and encourage the beauty of budding sexuality and the twinges of first love, she does not have, within her immediate world, any model of femininity. For there are only two women in *Hamlet*, both of whom are subservient to the male power system, and the chorus of courtiers consists entirely of male opportunists. There is no indication in the text that Claudius or any other of the men in this court are affected by Gertrude's obvious sensuality, for their attentions are concentrated more on political power than romance. Rather, it is Hamlet, the Orestean adolescent, whom we have already recognized as having an alien sense of values to the men of this court, that is troubled by and in need of mastering his attraction for his mother. Ophelia stands timidly at the threshold of womanhood but all of her first hopes, her first twinges of desire are cruelly nipped in the bud by her male guardians. Essentially the Ophelia/Electra character is reduced to an asexual tool of the male political system.

Within the Greek plays we have already recognized Electra as the repressed female principle within the Athenian male. To my mind Ophelia serves the identical function in *Hamlet*. We have already noticed that Hamlet's social self desperately wants to be convinced by the revenge-ideology of his day:

HAMLET

Witness this army of such mass and charge,
Led by a delicate and tender prince,
Whose spirit, with divine ambition puffed,
Makes mouths at the invisible event,
Exposing what is mortal and unsure
To all that fortune, death, and danger dare,
Even for an eggshell. Rightly to be great
Is not to stir without great argument,
But greatly to find quarrel in a straw
When honor's at the stake [4.4.49–58]

Yet despite these momentary bursts of patriotic enthusiasm, the enormous discrepancy between our hero's sensitive, reflective soul and the act of cold-blooded murder which he is called upon to exact constitutes the dialectics of the play. In order to harden himself to the act of revenge, it becomes essential for Hamlet to snuff out the more lyrical, feminine life-force within him. In this light, the devastating verbal cruelty which Hamlet inflicts on Ophelia (and which merely confirms for her the worldly cynicism with which she had been bombarded by her father and her brother at the beginning of the play) begins to be understood, for by destroying Ophelia, the feminine, he is ridding his soul of all moral compunctions in much the same manner as Agamemnon had sacrificed his virgin daughter, Iphigenia, to the all-male spirit of war:

HAMLET

. . . I did love you once.

OPHELIA

Indeed, my lord, you made me believe so.

HAMLET

You should not have believed me, for virtue cannot so inoculate our old stock but we shall relish of it. I loved you not.

OPHELIA

I was the more deceived.

HAMLET

Get thee to a nunnery! . . .
We are arrant knaves all; believe none of us. Go thy ways to a nunnery. Where's your father?

OPHELIA

At home, my lord.

HAMLET

Let the doors be shut upon him, that he may play the fool nowhere
but in's own house. Farewell.

. . .

If thou dost marry, I'll give thee this plague for thy dowry: be thou
as chaste as ice, as pure as snow, thou shalt not escape calumny. Get
thee to a nunnery. Go, farewell. Or if thou wilt needs marry, marry
a fool, for wise men know well enough what monsters you make of
them. . . To a nunnery, go, and quickly too. Farewell [3.1.131–150].

Shakespeare seems as aware as the Greek playwrights of the devastating effect that the repression of the female has on society, for Ophelia,
denied the maturing influence of a lover and the nurture of female council, sinks pathetically into the whirlpool of her imprisoned mind.

In *Hamlet*, it is the murdered lover that assumes the energizing
office held, in the time of the Greeks, by the ancient dead heroes.
Ophelia as gentle virgin, falls prey to a harsh, male reality, but Ophelia
as female archetype reemerges in the image of her open grave.
Ophelia's burial site, like the Greek burial mound, forces itself on
stage, grants the hero the experience of mourning, denied him at his
father's death, and thereby provides for him the necessary transition to
adulthood: the death and rebirth of Hamlet as hero. Only when he
physically immerses himself within the great mother as represented by
the open grave of Ophelia does Hamlet become part of the ancient
chain of ritual mourners, part of the cycle of death and rebirth that we
observed in ancient mythology. In the open grave of his denied love,
Hamlet dies and is reborn as hero. Thus the Hamlet-hero grows, like
the Aeschylean, out of the chrysalis of the feminine Ophelia-Electra.

Jan Kott says:

> From the end of the first scene of Act V, Hamlet is in the situation
> of Orestes, while through the first four acts he was in the situation of
> Electra—deprived of his rights, dependent on his father's murderer,
> threatened, like Electra, with exile or death.

Moreover, Kott claims that

> one can exactly define the point at which the real action of Orestes
> begins in Shakespeare's Hamlet. It is at the end of the first scene of
> Act V, when Hamlet jumps into Ophelia's grave. . . .[74]

Kott points out that from this point on the structure of the play changes. It observes the unities and assumes the structure of the classical tragedy. Viewed in this light, the Shakespearean protagonist becomes a hero, not when he destroys the feminine within him (as the male-hero of Western culture always seems to believe), but, on the contrary, when he reconciles himself with the very same feminine principle which, in his zeal for focus, clarity, and action, he has so cruelly destroyed.

It has been pointed out that Shakespeare was writing during England's adolescence. Could it be that he and the earlier Greek playwrights all foresaw the future demise of an empire that could sacrifice loyalty, remembrance and introspection in preference for action, power and political expediency?

But Shakespeare's idea of heroism is very different from that to which the "sane," the conscious and the socially-processed aspect of Hamlet aspires, and which characterizes the demonstrative bravery and mindless action of Fortinbras (Fort-en-bras, strong-in-arms) and Laertes. In this sense Shakespeare, as artist, follows in the path of the Greek poets, and again the spectators are forced to recognize a discrepancy between the ideology of the hero and that of the playwright. For Shakespeare, as Sophocles before him, recognizes that the underlying threat of Western civilization lies within the human soul as within the social structure.

Cole quotes Ionesco:

> Drama is one of the oldest of the arts. And I can't help thinking we cannot do without it. . . . To bring phantoms to life and give them flesh and blood is a prodigious adventure, so unique that I myself was absolutely amazed, during the rehearsals of my first play, when I suddenly saw, moving on the stage of the *Noctambules*, characters who owed their life to me. It was a terrifying experience. What right had I to do a thing like that? Was it allowed? . . . It was almost diabolical.[75]

Is it because modern man has separated his deities into God and the Devil that the "holy" evocation of the imagined has become so charged with ambivalence?

V

Electra: Play of Ambivalence

Ambivalence, irony, alienation, and the disjunction between surface and subtext have become the hallmarks of modern theater and, as
such, are themselves appropriate subject matter for the Electra myth:
the confrontation of the fragmented modern mind with the relative
certainty of a more classical worldview as the meeting and assessment
of the old by the new.

In *Madness in Literature*, Lilian Feder[76] traces madness, itself a
recurring theme in the Electra myth, to its earliest known literary form,
to the ancient Dionysian ritual that we find enacted within Euripides'
The Bacchae. The fifth-century experience of Dionysian rites, she
maintains, was not so much an expression of the ecstatic, as of the
already fully realized conflict between Apollonian (rational, masculine)
restraints and the human being's instinctual gravitation toward the
Dionysian (frenzied) life-force. The rites of Dionysus, maintains Feder,
reach back at least as far as the thirteenth century B.C., to a period when
the primordial person could not yet differentiate between him or
herself and objective reality. According to Feder, human existence at
that time was comprised solely of the ecstatic and the instinctual, a time
when the pleasure principle was not yet impeded by ego control.

According to this theory, the birth of civilization occurred when
the human being began to separate from his or her physical surround-
ings and to regard him or herself as an independent entity. It was at
that point that the human began to feel the need for stability and self-
regulation. Primordial rites and totem rituals became attempts on the
part of this newly enlightened creature to incorporate within itself some
of the principles that regulated the outer world. They became a way of
imbibing into human life, the strength and the surviving spirit of
nature. From a modern perspective, this effort of man and woman to
literally fill themselves with outer reality might well testify to an existential need even at that early period, an attempt to physically incorporate a sense of being into an otherwise devastatingly aching void.

Thus, from the very birth of civilization the rational human has

struggled with his or her chaotic, frenzied nature, the conflict itself producing its own madness: the madness of conflict superimposed upon
the madness of the untrammelled instinct.

Nietzsche idealized the Dionysian person. For Nietzsche, as for
Jung, it was Socrates who inflicted the curse of reason upon humankind, reason which over the ages has alienated men and women from
their true natures. Reason, according to Nietzsche, is not intrinsic to the
human being; rather, it is an arbitrary concept, a sort of Pirandellian
mask superimposed over and stifling one's basic life-force. In the
following chapter we shall see that in *Salome*, whose title character was
an immensely popular figure among artists at the turn of the twentieth
century, Oscar Wilde brought into direct confrontation the two extremes, the untrammable pleasure principle which since the time of the
Greeks has been depicted as the archetypal female, and the "masculine" principle of order so deadly in its distance from the vital life-juices
of human nature. It is a confrontation that obliterates the last vestiges
of civilization.

Nietzsche did acknowledge the fact that the human person would
never have survived, would have long fallen victim to his or her orgiastic
frenzies, if the Apollonian factor had not existed, in some form or
other, since earliest times. It is only in recognition of this that Nietzshe
reconciled himself to the necessity of human development within the
Apollonian factor.

Freud recognized the essential interdependence of the pleasure
principle with the human being's instinctive death-wish. According to
him, the instinct for destruction is intrinsically bound with that of survival. One destroys in order to devour, to imbibe, to be nourished and
to survive (a pattern that might again remind us of the ancient Earth
Mother or Mother Goddess). These are contradictions that have been
characteristic of the human person since his or her earliest attempts to
incorporate within him and herself the rhythms of winter-spring and
death and rebirth that are manifest within external reality. They are
instincts that again will be dramatized in Wilde's *Salome*. (I am conscious, as I write, that by according women their grammatical place
within the text, I am placing them back into history, evoking the
scream of the silence that women have held in the history of the human
race.)

Men and women swing eternally on their pendulum of reason and
madness, life and death. Nietzsche recognizes human redemption only
within the cruel frenzy of the pure life-force, within the human being's

regression to a pre–Oedipal state in which neither he nor she is subject to any superimposed governing body. According to Nietzsche, the Socratic rule, reason, and the Apollonian factor all represent the splintering of ourselves from our true natures to a distanced vantage point from which we attempt to administer control. Ironically, it is from this distance that we recognize the incompatibility of "masculine" control with the more "feminine," human aspects of human nature. It is from the vantage point of critical reasoning that we are forced to recognize the frailty and the pathos within the human condition, and it is from this distancing of ourselves from our true natures, from the double vision that we have thereby created, that the grotesque emerges. As for the irony that has become so characteristic of modern theater, it is the irony of the mirror, the irony of the artist who sees— from a third vantage point—how human nature is equally enslaved to passions and dedicated to control.

Thus we have recognized several layers of madness: the destructive, orgiastic, frenzy of our instincts (pre–Greek, pre–Hebraic chaos; the chaos of early Genesis); the madness created by the tension of opposites—life and death, instinct and reason, survival and destruction, love and hate; and, perhaps the ultimate madness, that of the "objective" vision, of being able, by means of reason, to observe the pathos of our human condition and the arbitrary nature of those qualities that we hold as absolutes—Heroism, Vengeance, and Honor. All these issues constitute the subject matter of the Electra plays of the twentieth century.

Yet the theme of madness extends even further, for it becomes emblematic of the splintered, alienating theater of the twentieth century, a theater which reflects the shattered, subjective reality that Kant portrays in his *Critique of Pure Reason*. Since Kant there is no Truth, no Reality, no shared experience. Reality is at best a momentary, shifting subjective matter, the awareness of which thrusts the individual even further into the loneliness and the separateness of his or her personal vision. Perhaps even that would not be so painful were it not that men and women suffer both from the hope that they are members of a community, and from the recognition that their hope is a delusion:

> ... I could be bounded in a nutshell, and count myself a king of infinite space, were it not that I have bad dreams [*Hamlet*: 2.2.270–272].

The latter half of nineteenth-century Austria can perhaps be regarded as a focal point of contemporary political reality. Cultural life blossomed. Art, music, theater, and especially opera flourished. The Conservative Party tried to preserve its elegant lifestyle for the upper classes and protect it from the contamination of the ambitious and threatening bourgeoisie, while the latter, consisting of merchants, Jews, and intellectuals, placed its faith in the Liberal Party, believing that Vienna could be enjoyed by all. The peasants and the lower classes, on the other hand, whom the Liberals had hoped to attract, identified more with the reactionary Catholic orthodoxy of the Conservatives. The National Socialist Party of Vienna headed by Karl Lueger was overtly anti–Semitic. Its assumption of political power in 1895 spelled the doom of the Liberal Party and saw the beginning of the moral, social, and political disintegration of Austria, and of the horrors of Europe as a whole.[77]

It is this moral disintegration and the effect it had upon society that concerns the playwrights and the artists of the twentieth century. The turn of the century, then, saw the beginning of what was to become an overt and mass disregard for human life, yet it is, at the same time, the age of Sigmund Freud, who devoted his life to the most minute and intricate workings of the mind of the individual. Carl Schorske, in his book *Fin-de-Siècle Vienna*, questions how two such disparate conceptions of human life could form within the same time and place.

It is relevant to mention Freud in this study because by means of his research on human psychology he irreversibly changed the human perception of reality, because his life is an excellent reflection of the intellectual mood and conflicts of his time, and because he both constitutes within his own life the prototypical Orestean experience and provides a model by means of which modern artists can challenge the creative form of their fathers.

Freud lived from 1856 to 1939. He was raised in a liberal Viennese Jewish family from which he watched the political development of his day. He identified strongly with the Dreyfus case in France and re-garded Emile Zola as his political hero because Zola had championed the Dreyfus cause. As a school boy he had idealized Napoleon as the conqueror and champion of a backward Central Europe. He admired England and the historical advances of Oliver Cromwell and he de-spised the aristocracy. Freud's father and friends set their hopes for an emancipated Austria on the Liberal Party. The young Sigmund himself had entertained hopes throughout his high school years of growing up to be a politician and of realizing his father's hopes for the future, within the Liberal Party. In 1895, however, the Nationalist Socialist Party came into power, thereby crushing the hopes of the liberals and reinstating an era of racial prejudice and social discord. The effects of anti–Semitism were widespread. Freud himself was squeezed out of a well-earned position within the respected upper class intellectuals of his day into the more urbane middle-class of Jewish medical practitioners. He even joined the B'nai B'rith, an international Jewish fraternity at this point, out of a need for social comfort and personal acceptance.

When Freud was ten or twelve years old, his father told him of an act of anti–Semitism which he had experienced as a boy. Sigmund was humiliated that his father had not responded, in any way, to such an attack on human dignity. He felt that his father had behaved un-heroically and had failed to live up to the principles of the Liberal Party which he had espoused. Years later, in an interesting transmutation of this incident, Freud recorded in his *Interpretation of Dreams* a dream in which Hannibal, the classical Roman conqueror, forced his son to swear before the altar that he would avenge the insults that his father had received at the hands of the Romans. It would seem that the increase of anti– Semitism during his lifetime had forced Freud, by means of the pattern of classical heroism, to avenge the humiliation of his father.

Sigmund's father died in 1896. Sigmund wrote that such a tragedy is "the most important event, the most poignant loss, of a man's life." He was painfully aware that his father had never realized his political aspirations. Schorske writes:

> To lay his father's ghost, Freud had either, like Hamlet, to affirm the primacy of politics by removing what was rotten in the state of Denmark (a civic task) or to neutralize politics by reducing it to psychological categories (an intellectual task).[78]

Thus we have the origins, perhaps, of Freud's revolutionary descent into the human mind. Schorske suggests that Europe's mass disregard for human life and for the individual may be the very cause of Freud's probings into the most minute and intricate workings of the individual psyche.

For a time the head of the National Socialist Party in Austria was led by an Austrian aristocrat by the name of Count Thun who became a controversial figure because of his constant struggle to unite two factions — the Hungarian and the Italian parties — which were threatening to disband. Schorske narrates that once, while waiting at a railway station, Freud witnessed an incident he no doubt considered typical of aristocratic arrogance on the part of Count Thun when the latter brushed aside the station-master, disclaimed the need to purchase a ticket, and established himself in a first class carriage, merely by virtue of his political prominence. At this, Freud's egalitarian feelings rose to the fore. "He found himself whistling a subversive air from Mozart's *Marriage of Figaro*: "If the Count wants to dance, I'll call the tune."[79] Schorske continues to say that on the train Freud slept and dreamt that he challenged Count Thun's arrogance and aristocratic political views. He dreamt that he saw his father straddling two chairs, thereby physically incorporating the two contentious parties, the Hungarians and the Italians, with which the Count was having such difficulties. In this way, Freud was performing the function of the previously mentioned Hannibal's son, that is, he was avenging the wrongs done to his father and reestablishing him in a position of political power. Schorske writes:

> In the dream he had discharged by his defiance of the Count, the commitment of his youth to anti-authoritarian political activism, which was also his unpaid debt to his father.

The third section of Freud's "Revolutionary Dream" (as related by Schorske) shows Freud's aging father at the railway station. In it Freud holds a urinal so that his father can relieve himself. In his analysis of this dream Freud recalls two childhood incidents in which his father had reprimanded him for relieving himself in public. On one of those occasions the father had been so incensed that he had shouted at Sigmund's mother that the boy would never amount to anything! In his dream, Freud is, at one and the same time, reestablishing his father in a position of power and avenging him of his childhood insult. Here, after his father's death, Sigmund is demonstrating to his father in dream form that he is successful and that he has mastery over him:

> From political encounter, through flight into academia, to the conquest of the father who has replaced Count Thun, patricide replaces regicide; psychoanalysis overcomes history. Politics is neutralized by a counterpolitical psychology.

In Freud's mind victory over one's father represents the victory over politics. He writes:

> The whole rebellious content of the dream, with its lese majeste and its derision of the higher authorities, went back to rebellion against my father. A prince is known as father of his country; the father is

the oldest, first and, for children, the only authority, and from his
autocratic power the other social authorities have developed in the
history of human civilization.

Schorske writes that Freud's Oedipal quest (which, in our case, we
might recognize as an Orestean quest) was "a moral and intellectual
one: to escape a fate and acquire self-knowledge." He says: "By reduc-
ing his own political past and present to an epiphenomenal status in
relation to the primal conflict between father and son, Freud gave his
fellow liberals an ahistorical theory of man and society that could make
bearable a political world spun out of orbit and beyond control."[80]
This, it seems to me, is the function of the Orestean hero.

Equally important to our understanding of modern theater is
Nietzsche. Nietzsche wrote in the tradition of Schopenhauer. He recognized that Europe at the end of the twentieth century was falling apart:
its institutions and its ways of living were becoming outmoded.
Nietzsche witnessed the dissolution of the ruling upper-middle class.
New ideas were rising to the fore: ahistoricity, the idea that men and
women should make a clean break from the past, from the patterns of
patriarchal society, that there should be a movement away from government and the family structure. The entire patriarchal structure was
called into question. Art, in a newly psychologized world, became the
one way to reach a truth that existed beyond history, beyond the accepted social-structure, even beyond logic, reason, and the linear use
of language.

Nietzsche, Freud, Ibsen, and Pirandello all entertained similar
ideas though they did not know one another and worked within
different disciplines. All four advocated the dissolution of power
politics and called into question the social mores of the time. Nietzsche
foresaw that the twentieth century would be a battleground of conflicting ideologies. It is interesting that as we near the end of the twentieth
century we are experiencing the same need for revolution as at the end
of the last century and the same issues are at stake: birth control,
women's rights, the need to redefine the respective roles of the male
and the female, and equitable treatment for homosexuals. There seems
to be a cyclical nature to certain intellectual concepts that are fundamental to Western culture. Nietzsche questioned the nature and existence of Truth. He looked for a new reality to replace the outmoded
historical perspective. He questioned the nature of existence. What is
the human condition? What does it mean to be alive? What is the
nature and purpose of human reality? As had Hegel seventy-five years

earlier, Nietzsche preached that God is dead. He believed that the general public was clinging to an obsolete concept for it was living "in the shadows of the dead god." He believed that they should overcome their dependence on a paternalistic culture that no longer represents reality. He knew that the twentieth century would become a battleground for simultaneous but disparate ideologies.

Oscar Wilde: *Salome* (1905)

Oscar Wilde belonged to the Aesthetic Movement at the turn of the century, believing that the function of art was not to recreate reality, but to create art for art's sake. Wilde was not interested in linear progression, in cause and effect. Rather, he concentrated all aspects of his theater on one point in time, on one focal point of heightened dramatic tension. Above all else, his theater was sensual. For him an exploration and a revolution of the senses provided the necessary access to reality. To this end, perfume was sprayed liberally throughout the house during the performances of his play. By means of his repetitive, hypnotic use of language, his poetry, his use of alliteration and his symbolism, his concentration on the decadent, on the mystical and the macabre, Wilde, the ultimate symbolist, created a world of fantasy and dream, the validity of which can be traced only to the inner recesses of the subconscious. As such, the Orestean figure of Oscar Wilde confronted the old theater of linear form and rational meaning with the inner, dream-like sensuality of a new generation.

Again, the explosion of the inner sensuality and life-force is presented in the irrepressible female form. Salome is chaste, cold and deadly as the moon. Like the moon she is hypnotic. Like the moon she brings madness, passion and death:

PAGE OF HERODIAS

Look at the moon! How strange the moon seems! She is like a woman rising from a tomb. She is like a dead woman. You would fancy she was looking for dead things[81]

THE YOUNG SYRIAN

She has a strange look. She is like a little princess who wears a yellow veil, and whose feet are of silver. She is like a princess who has little white doves for feet...

PAGE OF HERODIAS

She is like a woman who is dead. She moves very slowly [319].

Salome is erotic love. She is the Id, willful and irrepressible. In the single shaft of the moon shining on the stage Salome is crushed between the shields of the soldiers. It takes the congregated army of the king to extinguish the threat of sexuality.

The play luxuriates in the sensuousness of death, decay and eroticism. It is the sensuousness of Electra, this time — a Judaean princess, young, mysterious and distant as the virginal moon. Again we see her as a projection of the male phantasy.

Wilde's play is filled with the complexity, with the heightened sounds and colors of the Orient, and with the suggestion of danger lurking within the shadows:

SALOME

. . . barbarians who drink and drink, and spill their wine on the pavement, and Greeks from Smyrna with painted eyes and painted cheeks, and frizzed hair curled in twisted coils, and silent, subtle Egyptians, with long nails of jade and russet cloaks, and Romans brutal and coarse, with their uncouth jargon [322].

It is filled with the sensuality of *The Song of Songs*, a sensuality that forms the subtext of the *Book of Prophets* for it is a deliberate attempt on the part of the poet to reach beyond Christianity, to strip the Bible of the Puritan straitjacket that has been thrust upon it by modernity.

SALOME

Jokanaan, I am amorous of thy body! Thy body is white like the lilies of a field that the mower hath never mowed. Thy body is white like the snows that lie on the mountains, like the snows that lie on the mountains of Judaea, and come down into the valleys. The roses in the garden of the Queen of Arabia are not so white as thy body. Neither the roses in the garden of the Queen of Arabia, the perfumed garden of spices of the Queen of Arabia, nor the feet of the dawn when they light on the leaves, nor the breast of the moon when she lies on the breast of the sea. . . . There is nothing in the world so white as thy body. Let me touch thy body.
. . .
. . . It is of thy hair that I am enamored, Jokanaan. Thy hair is like clusters of grapes, like the clusters of black grapes that hang from the vine trees of Edom in the land of the Edomites. Thy hair is like the cedars of Lebanon, like the great cedars of Lebanon that give their

shade to the lions and to the robbers who would hide themselves by
day. The long black nights, when the moon hides her face, when the
stars are afraid, are not so black [327].

In this play the image of the moon stands in opposition to that of
the people. Wilde deliberately creates the dialectics of pagan ritual versus Christianity as the Dionysian versus the Apollonian. Like the theme
of the virgin–Electra that we have noted thus far, the fascination of
Jokanaan lies in his inaccessibility. There is a hypnotic rhythm even to
the severity of the prophet:

JOKANAAN

Daughter of Sodom, come not near me! But cover thy face with a veil,
and scatter ashes upon thine head, and get thee to the desert and seek
out the Son of Man.

SALOME

Who is he, the Son of Man? Is he as beautiful as thou art, Jokanaan?

JOKANAAN

Get thee behind me! I hear in the palace the beatings of the wings
of the angel of death.
. . .
Back! daughter of Babylon! By woman came evil into the world.
Speak not to me. I will not listen to thee. I listen but to the voice of
the Lord God [327].

From a post–Puritan perspective, Woman is synonymous with the
devil. Jokanaan (John the Baptist), on the other hand, is the prophet
of the loving figure of Jesus, yet he is represented as totally antithetical
to him in nature, as rigid and vindictive. Does Wilde depict him in this
way as a means of demonstrating society's misunderstanding of Christianity? Is he saying that the denial of the senses, which is the purpose
of both Christian and Apollonian austerity, necessitates the abolition
of love? All the poets within our study recognize a necessary relationship between sensual freedom and the love of the heart. Wilde maintains that puritan Christianity does not.

Simultaneously, on the same stage, we are presented with Jokanaan
and his rejection of the sensual and with the savage paganism of the
Nubian gods, deities that rip men to shreds and revel in their destruction:

THE NUBIAN

The gods of my country are very fond of blood. Twice a year we sacrifice to them young men and maidens; fifty young men and a hundred maidens. But it seems we never give them quite enough, for they are very harsh to us [320].

In her deadly dance of the seven veils, Electra reveals to its fullest the beauty and violence of pagan sensuality.

This Judaean princess is the indomitable Electra who subverts the law for her own gratification, yet who is held against her will beneath the lecherous gaze of her uncle-stepfather. Jokanaan is the Orestes, brought up out of the bowls of the earth by his sister-lover. What is dramatized here is the attraction of opposites and the human fascination for the forbidden fruit, again an ironic blend of Christian and pagan themes. Salome is tied to Jokanaan, dramatically, by means of color. The moon is silver. Salome's hands and feet are white like a dove's and the body of Jokanaan assumes an ivory tinge as he emerges from the pit in which he has been held (itself an image of death and rebirth that is ironic in its similarity to the ancient rites of passage described earlier in this work). These two opposites are bound also by the redness of roses and pomegranates associated with *The Song of Songs* and the land of Judea, by the redness of blood and violence, of Salome's lips and the tongue of Jokanaan:

SALOME

It is thy mouth that I desire, Jokanaan. Thy mouth is like a band of scarlet on a tower of ivory. It is like a pomegranate cut with a knife of ivory. The pomegranate-flowers that blossom in the gardens of Tyre, and are redder than roses, are not so red. The red blasts of trumpets that herald that approach of kings, and make afraid the enemy, are not so red. Thy mouth is redder than the feet of those who tread the wine in the wine-press. Thy mouth is redder than the feet of the doves who haunt the temples and are fed by the priests. It is redder than the feet of him who cometh from a forest where he hath slain a lion, and seen gilded tigers. Thy mouth is like a branch of coral that fishers have found in the twilight of the sea, the coral that they keep for the kings! . . . It is like the vermilion that the Moabites find in the mines of Moab, the vermilion that the kings take from them. . . . There is nothing in the world so red as thy mouth. . . . Let me kiss thy mouth [328].

The language that ties them is filled with the exotic riches of the earth and with the violence and rapaciousness of kings. It is at once biblical, cruel, and erotic.

Herod Antipas is the tetrarch of Judaea. Like Claudius, he has murdered his brother in order to take for himself the queen of Judaea. He is the representation of Roman, secular law and his function is to subjugate the disparate factions of Judaea under the canopy of the Roman Empire. As such he is recognizable to us as the repressive and myopic Aegisthus. Jokanaan represents divine law, the law of the spiritual fathers. He is called from the pit (as in Aeschylus' play) by the figure of Electra. It is Jokanaan's word (spirit) and the action (dance) of Salome combined, which constitute defiance and which bring about the downfall of Herod and Herodias. It is the combined actions of Electra and Orestes that bring about the liberation of the realm.

The religious law represented by Jokanaan is overruled by the civil law of the Roman tetrarch, yet ultimately secular power is also overthrown because of the tetrarch's fidelity to his word:

HEROD

Ah! Wherefore did I give my oath? Kings ought never to pledge their word. If they keep it not, it is terrible, and if they keep it, it is terrible also [345].

Ultimately, the overwhelming law of the play is neither politics nor religion, but sexuality. In a manner reminiscent of Macbeth, the tetrarch attempts to extinguish the fires of conscience and sexuality and hide beneath the canopy of power and possession:

HEROD

Put out the torches! Hide the moon! Hide the stars! Let us hide ourselves in our palace, Herodias. I begin to be afraid [347].

With the bombardment of the senses that we have witnessed in this play, Wilde has dealt with sexuality as the aesthetes had dealt with art. On his stage, sexuality is no longer the subtext of theater, but, to put it as bluntly as he does, "sex for sex sake." By this means he forces his spectators to confront all the credos by which they live: their sexuality, their humanitarianism and the purpose and function of their religion.

Hugo von Hofmannsthal: *Electra* (1903)

Hofmannsthal says of Friedrich Hebbel's poetry that it

penetrates us in such a way that the most secret . . . inner depths stir
in us and the actually demonic, the natural in us, sounds in dark and
intoxicating sympathetic vibration.[83]

While attempting to describe the creative dilemmas of the aristocratic
and liberal aesthetes and artists of fin-de-siècle Vienna, Schorske writes
that "the instinctual element in man . . . provided the power whereby
one could escape from the prison of aestheticism, from the paralysis of
narcissistic sensibility."[84] Hofmannsthal felt that engagement in life

> demands the capacity to resolve, to will. This capacity implies com-
> mitment to the irrational, in which alone resolution and will are
> grounded. Thus affirmation of the instinctual reopened for the
> aesthete the door to the life of action and society.

He added:

> The nature of our epoch, is multiplicity and indeterminacy. It can
> rest only on *"das Gleitende"* (the moving, the slipping, the sliding),
> and is aware that what other generations believed to be firm is in fact
> "das Gleitende."[85]

Hofmannsthal was not unaware of Freud and his controversial theories
of sexual, emotional and political repression. He was only too aware of
the dynamics of repressed emotions within his own society and
recognized within these dynamics, as did many artists of that period,
an untapped form of artistic expression, one that had not already been
worn threadbare by traditional use and which he grasped for himself
as the one means by which to combat both the insipid and inertia-
bound aestheticism of the aristocracy, and the stifling hold that
religious mores and ethics wielded over the middle, and lower-classes.
Of Hofmannsthal's *Der Turm*, Schorske writes, "Where law ignores
instinct, instinct rebels and subverts order. Politics is here psychologized, psychology politicized."[86] Turn of the century Vienna was a
period in which the old vanguard of Catholic aristocracy was no longer
able to withstand the threat of the Liberal Party, and both constituen-
cies were in constant competition from the Social Democrats and the
Pan-Germans for their moment of political power. Hofmannsthal, as
an intellectual of his time and as the grandson of a member of the
Jewish bourgeoisie who had been granted membership by the Emperor
himself into the then much coveted aristocracy, was only too aware of
the dangerous anti–Semitic agitation of such social and political
climbers as Georg von Schonerer and Karl Lueger, precursors and
ideologues for no less a danger than Adolf Hitler and Nazi Europe.

Like the Renaissance and the Jacobean societies, fin-de-siècle Vienna
was a quicksand of class disintegration and social instability, and, in
this case, it fostered the most insidious and volatile forms of political
insurrection.

From within this pattern the figure of Electra emerges, again as a
force of violence commensurate with the degree to which she has been
repressed. The emphasis in this play is not on Orestes, the heroic-
masculine instrument of right and retribution. On the contrary,
Orestes appears here as little more than a boy trembling in a lonely,
godless world at the act he is about to commit:

ELECTRA

I've never seen the gods, and yet I'm certain
that they will be here with you, they will help you.

ORESTES

I do not know the gods, but I know this:
they have laid this deed upon my conscience,
and they will scorn me if I tremble at it.[87]

He appears as a lad, forced into action by the living horror of his sister
and the act of violence that has possessed her since early childhood:

ORESTES

Does our mother look like you in any way?

ELECTRA

Like me? No. I will not
have you look her in the face. When she is dead,
then we together will look her in the face.
O my brother, she threw a white shirt
upon our father, and then she struck away
at that which stood before her, helpless, sightless,
which could not turn its face to hers, whose arms
could not work free — are you listening to me?
she struck down at this with her axe raised high
above him [110–1].

The masculine principle here is but a timid child, a product of Electra's
need. In a society of such despotism and such repressed violence, as that
of fin-de-siècle Europe, there can be no masculine heroism, only an
Electra, the volcanic eruption of a long over-repressed female principle.

The heroine here serves as the agent of liberation in an essentially amoral world, a world which does not rotate on a scale of right and wrong, but of repression and liberation. This is not an aesthetically self-reflective world, but one that explodes from imprisonment into violent action. In this play, then, in stark contrast to that of Sophocles on which it is patterned, Electra is not merely the female pattern of lyricism, remembrance and inertia, but also the embodiment of "the deed" of enfranchisement as a direct reaction to her enslavement. She is the driving, underlying force of demonic energy that propels the play into action. The "deed," the act of revenge, constitutes her very *raison d'être*:

ELECTRA

Happy the man who does! Who dares to do!
A deed is like a bed on which the soul
can rest, a bed of balsam where the soul
that is a wound, a blight, a running sore,
a sore that flames like fire!
. . .
. . . When I was steeped in hatred
I kept nothing but silence. Hatred is nothing,
it consumes itself, and love is still less
than hatred, it grasps out at everything,
but fastens onto nothing, its hands are like flames
that cannot grasp; and thought, too, is nothing,
and all that comes from our mouths is feeble air:
that man alone is happy who comes to do!
And happy who dares to touch him and who digs
his axe from the earth, who holds the torch for him,
who opens the door, who listens there [111].

Electra here is the daemon that infests all the other characters with her spirit and provokes them into action. Thus when Chrysothemis tells her sister of the terrible dream that their mother had had, Electra cries out:

ELECTRA

I! I!
I sent it to her. I sent her this dream
from my own breast! I lie in bed and hear
the footsteps of the spectre haunting her.
I hear him make his way from room to room
and lift the curtain from her bed: screaming
she leaps from the bed, but he is always there,
close behind her on the stairs, the chase continues
from one vault to another and another.

It is far darker now than any night,
far quieter and darker than the grave,
she gasps and staggers in darkness, but he is there:
he swings the torch to right and left of the axe.
And I like a hunting-hound am at her heels:
should she hide in a hollow, I spring after,
sideways, upon her trail, and drive her on
till a wall end her flight, and there in darkness,
there in deepest darkness—I see him still,
his shadow, and his limbs, the light of his eyes—
there sits our father, who neither sees nor hears,
and yet, it must happen; we drive her to his feet,
and the axe falls! [93-4].

Electra is the daemon that weaves a "sinister dance" around Aegisthus
as she herds him into his death-chamber, and at the end of her play
when Chrysothemis runs joyously to her sister with the news of their
liberation—"and rejoice;/ a thousand torches are lighted. Don't you
hear it?"—Electra, the demonic spirit, responds with:

ELECTRA

Don't I hear it? Hear the music?
That music comes from me. Those thousands and thousands
with torches, they whose boundless myriad footsteps
make hollow rumbling round the earth, all these,
these, wait upon me: I know that they all,
all, wait upon me to lead the dance [113].

Electra is witchlike, maniacal. Her insanity is the stuff of revolution and of theater; it explodes from the inside out, and refuses to
recognize any authority. She is the tumultuous, volcanic force of the
repressed female. She burns herself out in a frenzy of insanity, yet it
is her insane, essentially theatrical magic that produces the hero. Electra
dies for the birth of Chrysothemis. Her dance becomes the web of the
black mother-spider herself. It is the relentlessly historical dance of
death and rebirth which holds the actors and the audience in one
magnetic center. Modern dramatists have directed their attention to
the question of the bourgeois audience and its lack of intrinsic relationship to the theatrical act, yet there is no need here to stimulate the audience in an Artaudian fashion with momentary emotional stimuli. Nor
is there a need to alienate the spectators into political reflection or
separate thought patterns. This vortex of hatred and expiated passion
constitutes in and of itself the theatrical event as it is defined by David
Cole: "Theatre does not serve purposes; it has a purpose: to bring us the

presence of imaginative events. . . . 'interpretation'—is ultimately a refusal of the theatrical event itself."[88] There is need for the irrational frenzy of violence within the context of freedom and theater, and in this—the protagonist's long-awaited dance of life and liberation—Electra spins herself out:

ELECTRA

Be silent and dance. All must come!
All must join with me! I bear the burden
of joy, and I dance here before you all.
One thing alone remains for him who is happy:
to be silent and dance! [114].

Despite the protagonist's earlier efforts, human experience cannot be understood within the logic-oriented harness of verbal expression. Ultimately, it is the irrational world of instincts that propels human behavior. The joy of liberation and the pain of the sacrifice it demands can be realized only within silence and dance. Thus, for Electra as for Hamlet, "silence is all." In a manner reminiscent of Shakespeare's Ophelia or of Goethe's Faust—the hero that so desperately sought to reconcile himself with the female opposition—Electra, the female figure of loyalty and remembrance, drowns within the waters of the feminine principle:

ELECTRA

. . . the ocean, the monstrous ocean,
the manifold ocean weighs me down with its burden
in every limb; I cannot lift myself! [114].

In our previous chapter, we had noted an evolution from the world of ritual that had characterized the grave-oriented work of Aeschylus' *Libation Bearers* to that of the more formal religion of Sophocles' *Electra*, in which Clytemnestra had prayed to Apollo, the masculine god of light and reason. In the present play, we are propelled into the twentieth century, a man-centered world, characterized more by anxiety and superstition than by dependence on any outer force. In this world, there are no determining forces. Calamities happen by chance, even the murder of Agamemnon is presented more as an error in timing than as a deliberate act of treachery:

CLYTEMNESTRA

. . . There are customs. Yes,
there must be customs, usages for all things.

> How one articulates a word or sentence can make much
> difference. Even the hour it's spoken.
> And whether one's fed or fasting. Many a man
> has perished for entering too soon into his bath [96].

In this world the gods are deaf and blind and people clutch desperately
at any straw for an answer to their ignorance. Here it is not Apollo but
the demented Electra who stands center-stage and to whom
Clytemnestra prays:

CLYTEMNESTRA

> I do not know them who play this game with me,
> whether they are at home above or below,
> but when I see you standing there before me
> as now you are, I cannot but believe
> but you are in league with them. Who are you really?
> Why can't you speak, now, when I would hear you? [97].

Religion is closed to the modern consciousness. In its place are
desperate, blind attempts at the occult:

ELECTRA

> Are you thinking of my father?

CLYTEMNESTRA

> That is why
> I am so behung with jewels. In every one
> exists a certain power. One must but know
> how to use them [96].

In her confusion Clytemnestra, the mother, reels pathetically from
dependence to despotism. In the absence of a god, Clytemnestra, the
queen, prays to her enslaved daughter whose very power lies in the force
of her enmity:

CLYTEMNESTRA

> ... If it were your pleasure,
> I know that you could tell me how to use them.

ELECTRA

> I, mother, I?

CLYTEMNESTRA

Yes, you! For you are wise.
Your mind is sound. You talk of old things
as if they happened yesterday. But I
decay. I think, but all things are confused.
And when I start to speak, Aegisthus cries,
and what he cries out is hateful to me,
and then I would rise up and would be stronger
than all his words, but I find nothing, nothing! [96].

There are no absolutes within the world of this play. Nothing is
secure. The gods are arbitrary and unrecognizable. Human, even
family relationships are suspect, and Aegisthus is reduced from the
status of lover to that of a weak and hated bedfellow. Reality, like
quicksand, is *Gleitende*.

The elegant theater-goers of fin-de-siècle Vienna attended the performance of this play no doubt to be entertained, to watch passively as
the players acted on stage. Yet the reality of the performance proved,
as do most realities, to be far different from the expected. Instead of
entertainment, the spectators are bombarded by pre-expressionistic
images of sound and sight. The stage is filled with symbols of blood,
of overripe, wasted sexuality, and of death and physical decay. Pitiful
cries of slave women wailing jackal-like in the night air, furtive, sadistic
sounds of whips lashing over bent bodies, shuffling of reluctant feet,
of women and of beasts being dragged off to sacrifice, and the constant
play of light and darkness, of hope and despair, uncertainty, mystery
and fear. All of these combine to crack the veneer of complacency with
which the spectators have entered this theater and overwhelm them
with the unverbalized, demonic world of the instincts pulsating beneath the varnish of external reality.

Clytemnestra appears on stage in the mummified guise of the eternal despot, a wasted figure, dredged of life, purpose and desire. Her
life-blood has been drained from her deathly white complexion to the
outer trappings of her garb, gaudy baubles, symbols of royalty and
decadence. The director is told:

> The figure of Clytemnestra appears in the wide window. Her sallow,
> bloated face, in the light thrown from the glaring torches, appears
> even more pale above her scarlet dress. She supports herself upon one
> of her women, dressed in dark violet, and upon an ivory staff
> embellished with precious jewels. Her train is carried by a yellow
> figure, whose black hair is combed back like an Egyptian, and whose

> sleek face resembles a poised snake. The queen is almost completely
> covered with precious stones and talismans. Her arms are full of
> bracelets, her fingers almost rigid with rings. The lids of her eyes seem
> excessively large, and it appears to be a great effort for her to hold
> them open [94].

She is, in fact, none other than the prehistoric Egyptian mother goddess. The snake that we had seen in Aeschylus' play as symbol of the
mother's ambivalence toward her son and as a projection onto him of
her own innermost fears has here become the emblem and the staff of
the queen herself; its venom is as deadly to her own person as it is to
her children. She is a personification of the horror and the decadence
of turn-of-the-century Europe. With his sumptuous repetition and
contrast of colors, gems, and textures (the red-blue hues of blood and
of the Queen's gown as they are mirrored in her heavy jewels), and with
his wax-like, ghostly interplay of the yellow tinge of the lighted torches
and candles as they reflect onto the ivory staff and the face of Clytemnestra's serpentine maidservant, Hofmannsthal seems to be borrowing
the gorgeously erotic art of the popular and controversial artist Gustav
Klimt and subverting it into grotesque images of horror, of death-
within-life and of human waste. Again we might cast our minds back
to the language and imagery of the biblical *Song of Songs*, and
recognize our fall from the ecstatic and the beautiful to the grotesque.
Suzanne Bales describes how, in a manner reminiscent of the Ghost of
Hamlet, Max Reinhardt (for whom this play was written) manipulated
the colors and the light and shadow in such a way as to create the
presence of Agamemnon on stage.[90]
   It is the erotic principle that constitutes the underlying energy and
determines the relationships within this play. Hofmannsthal was
specific in his directions for the stage: a sprawling fig-tree overhanging
the women's house of imprisonment laden with overripe fruit, fer-
menting figs strewn over the stage floor and the stage itself, bathed in
pools of blood and overripe, wasting sexuality. Because the protagonist
is so enslaved to the principle of hatred, because she has, in fact,
become transformed into the very figure of Hatred, she is unable to
realize her feminine, reproductive identity, the principle of life. In this
sense she is again Electra, the un-mated. Electra's reunion with her
brother has erotic undertones. With him, the first loving male to enter
her world, she is reminded of her ruined femininity and the audience
is granted a glimpse of the way life could have been, even for Electra,
had she not been traumatized by a sick and loveless world:

ELECTRA

Who
am I, that you should cast such loving looks
at me? See, I am nothing. All I was
I had to sacrifice: even that modesty,
that sweetest thing of all, which, like the silvery,
milky haze of the moon, hovers about
a woman and protects her and her soul
from all things horrible!l My modesty
was sacrificed as though I'd fallen among thieves
who stripped my last garment from me! I have
known the wedding-night, as no other virgins,
have known the pangs of women who bear children,
but have brought nothing into the world, nothing;
I have become a perpetual prophetess,
and have brought nothing forth from my body
except eternal curses and despair [110].

Electra, who has aged and hardened before her time, stands in sharp, dramatic contrast to the fullness and gentleness of her sister Chrysothemis—principle of life, love and fruition. Electra sacrifices life, for she is the conscience and the watchman of her generation. In an uncanny way, she foreshadows both the violence that was soon to rip apart Hofmannsthal's Europe and people like Simon Wiesenthal and Elie Wiesel, those watchmen of remembrance who have devoted their lives in our times to perpetuating the lesson of the European holocaust and to hunting down its perpetrators.

Again we might recall Hamlet's vow that he will remember the ghost of his father:

ELECTRA

Forget? Forget?
Am I a beast then that I should forget?
The beast will sleep with its half-eaten prey
hanging from its jaws; the beast forgets itself
and starts to chew, the while death sits on him,
strangling out life; the beast forgets what crept
from its own body, and with its own young
allays its hunger—I am no beast, I cannot forget! [92].

Electra is the epitome of the tragic hero in her relentless singleness of purpose:

ELECTRA

At night I never slept, but made my bed
high in the tower and cried down to the court

and whimpered with the dogs. I have hated,
I have seen everything, have had to see everything
just like the watchman on the tower,
and day is night and night becomes day again,
and I have found no joy in sun or stars,
for all things, for his sake, were nothing to me,
all things were but signs, and every day
a marker on the road [110].

Memory, in this sense, is synonymous with the principle of death. In a world in which the gods are indifferent to human suffering, the relentless vigil of the tragic heroine becomes, Antigone-like, the only exorciser of evil:

ELECTRA

... this time is given you
to know the fear that shipwrecked men must know
when their vain cry gnaws at the dark clouds
and the blackness of death; this time is given you
to envy those chained to prison walls,
those who cry out from the bottom of a well
for death as though for deliverance; for you,
you lie so prisoned up within yourself
as though in the glowing body of a beast
of bronze and, just as now, you cannot cry out!
And I stand there beside you, and your eyes
can never leave me, for you hope in vain
to read that word upon my silent face;
you roll your eyes, you'd grasp at any thought,
you'd have the gods smile down at you from the clouds;
but the gods, the gods are at supper, just as when
you slew our father, they're sitting there at supper
and are just as deaf now to any death-rattle!
Only a half-mad god, the god of laughter,
staggers in; he thinks it's all a game,
a love-game that you're playing with Aegisthus,
but when he sees his error, he laughs at once,
loud and shrill, and vanishes like that [100–1].

Electra and Chrysothemis are mirror-images of the same personality which merges and splits asunder, thereby impelling the action into the final climactic sacrifice and demise of Electra for the emancipation of Chrysothemis and her fellow prisoners:

ELECTRA

... and here I stand and see you
die at last! You will dream no longer then,

and I will dream no more, and who lives after,
let him rejoice and be happy in his life! [101].

Electra represents the death-wish, the destructive aspect of nature,
Physis, vengeance and remembrance, attributes that we have thus far
characterized as "feminine." She perhaps exemplifies Freud's theory of
history as a force that is propelled by an endless chain of violent erup-
tions, for she embodies the natural and perhaps cyclical movement
toward violence and release that forms the basis of historical action as
well as of theater. She is the personification of hatred that spins itself
into self-destruction and hers is the tragic death that is the precursor
of life in a terrifying prophecy of European history.

Chrysothemis, on the other hand, represents the benign, regen-
erative, yet somewhat apathetic and, by definition, unheroic life principle:

CHRYSOTHEMIS

... Before I die
I want to know what life is! I want children
before my body withers, and even though
they marry me with a peasant, I will bear him
children and will warm them with my body
through cold nights when storms beat at our hut! [91].

Claude Levi Strauss claims that tragedy is the result of relationships that are either strangulating in their proximity or that suffer from
too great an alienation. He writes:

> The overrating of blood relations is to the underrating of blood rela-
> tions as the attempt to escape autochthony is to the impossibility to
> succeed in it.[91]

It is interesting to note that Hofmannsthal constructs his play by
means of a series of such strained, parasitical dualities. Electra and
Orestes are siblings whose kinship is laced with unnaturally erotic
undertones. Electra is the violent force of repressed anger and her
brother, conjured by her in an Aeschylean fashion, is but the instrument and expression of her will. Aegisthus is described by Electra as
"the other woman," who is "too narrow around the chest" (95) to wear
her father's clothes. Clytemnestra, whom we have already recognized
as a grotesque mask of political power, decayed female sexuality and
pathetic vulnerability, is thus paired with an image of emasculation, no
more than a woman in man's clothing, who yet seems to be draining

her of her own life-force. The absence of any positive masculine ideal
is conspicuous throughout this play. Electra and Chrysothemis, on the
other hand, are chained together as mirror-images of the same being.

CHRYSOTHEMIS

> It's you who have bound me here
> with hoops of iron. Were it not for you,
> they would not keep us here. Were it not for your hate,
> for your unsleeping and excessive temper,
> which makes me tremble, they would not keep us
> locked and chained here in this prison, sister! [91].

They are as symbiotically intertwined as life and death. Electra, the
principle of vengeance, robbed of her last hope of deliverance, coils
herself physically around the body of her sister in her effort to impreg-
nate her with her hatred. With utmost desperation, Electra pledges
herself as midwife to Chrysothemis' unborn children in return for her
help in the necessary act of revenge. Viktor Auburtin described this
moment in the Max Reinhardt production in the following way:

> ... the most beautiful moment in the piece is when Electra kneels
> before her sister and begs her with gentle, sweet, ingratiating words
> to help kill her own mother.[92]

Here again, Eros is the daemon that motivates the action, and here
again, as in Sophocles' play, Electra has become Clytemnestra. In this
case she is the snake that entwines herself around those she should love
in her attempt to infest them with her venom. As with Aeschylus, the
snake here represents the "boundary-ambiguity," which "appears in
connection with the boundary between life and death, consciousness
and unconsciousness, male and female."[93] Suzanne Bales points out
that Electra's attack against her sister is an illustration of the enormous
sexual frustration from which she is suffering. As we had seen earlier,
"the sexual organs receive serpentine associations primarily because
copulation blurs the boundaries of the organism"[94]:

ELECTRA

> I'll hold you! With my wretched withered arms
> I'll wind about your body, and if you resist
> the knot is pulled tighter; I'll twist myself
> like tendrils round your body, sink my roots
> deep inside you and engraft my will
> into your blood! [104].

It is with uncanny insight that Hofmannsthal recognizes and pinpoints the turning point between memory as the province of one's moral conscience and that kind of often pseudonationalist poisonous hatred, borne of despair and supreme frustration, that threatens to destroy life itself.

ELECTRA

I will not let you go.
We two must grow like one, so that the knife
that severs both our bodies will bring death
... at once, for we are alone now in this world.
Out of your chaste strong mouth a terrible cry
must come, a cry as terrible as that
of the Death goddess ... [104].

And in an act that parallels and is directly antithetical to the act of creation, Electra breathes death into the body of her sister:

ELECTRA

I'll hold you here
till you have sworn to me, mouth upon mouth,
that you will help me [104].

Ultimately, the generative life-principle is antithetical to the principle of death and Electra is unable to hold on to her sister. Like Aeschylus' heroine, even like Hamlet, Electra here has to move into a liminal space, a space beyond life in order to bring the spirit of the past into the present. Like Aeschylus' heroine, and like Hamlet (when he jumps into the grave of Ophelia), Electra claws at the earth (the oldest symbol of life and fertility) with her bare hands and resurrects the spirit of her father in the form of Orestes. For Hofmannsthal, as for Aeschylus and Shakespeare, dynamic action is the direct result of the protagonist's contact with the past.

Richard Strauss: *Elektra* (1909)

Strauss was inspired by the Max Reinhardt production of Hofmannsthal's play, particularly by Reinhardt's musicality and natural sense of rhythm, into adapting the play to his own musical opera score. To this end, much of the written text has been forfeited by the composer in favor of his own musical language. Strauss introduces musical motifs to indicate specific atmospheres, time periods and characters. Thus much of the verbal struggle and mutual incriminations of the original text have been replaced by the composer with musical moods. In this presentation of the myth, Clytemnestra responds with an aching nostalgia to Electra's prompting. She reaches back into her past with a longing that for one brief moment almost bridges the gap between the mother and the daughter, and which illustrates the deep, unspoken need that each has for the other. Yet Suzanne Bales points out that, as the queen reaches back hungrily to her former self, the motif that is associated with Agamemnon is introduced in a beguiling and excruciatingly painful manner, suggesting that Clytemnestra is unable to regain her innocence. Past memories evoke both the good and the bad; her effort to regain her former innocence necessitates also her confrontation with her worst nightmare, that which she is struggling against with all her might, her own ghastly act of murder. Thus music, the language of emotion, has taken the place of the spoken word for the expression of the irrational, of those powerful emotions that underlie reality and which Hofmannsthal suggests are the cause of rebellion and violence.

Here again the action takes place in an all-female world, a world in which heroism, in the figure of the murdered king, is but a painful memory that most try to avoid. Orestes appears again, only at the end of the action, as a timid, waiting youth, as the prehero, as one that is conjured up again by Electra, the priestess, and goaded into the painful action that manhood in such a world exacts. Here again the stage represents the outer court of the women's prison. It is an area of violence, of darkness, of suspicion and of lurking shadows. It becomes the passage through which beasts of burden and human slaves pass on their way to the sacrificial altar, and, as such, it suggests the endless chain of violence and murder that characterizes human behavior today and has done so since time immemorial. It is the haunting-ground of Electra, perpetual mourner of the dead.

It is in this space that the chorus of slave women and female overseers open the action of the play. The difference between this chorus and those of Aeschylus and Sophocles is that the slaves of the earlier plays had agitated for liberation, while these women are agents of reactionism and despotism who work to repress any expression of freedom. As such, they appear in much more sinister form than the slave women of ancient Greece. They gossip about Electra with vindictive malice while at the same time providing us with a vivid account of

the protagonist's own fiery temperament and hostility toward them—
the slavewomen who represent the establishment and the world of this
play. This Electra is the perfect example of Northrop Frye's definition
of the tragic hero as one who is essentially estranged from society.[95]
Within a few lines it becomes obvious that our protagonist is an out-
cast, alienated in a world of savagery in which even the slave that
defends her thinks only in terms of hatred and cruelty. Electra's
madness is the madness of political and moral isolation. The sadism of
the chorus provides a grotesque mirror-image of the protagonist's
madness and also of the insanity of a decadent body politic.

The tragic heroine enters at dusk, the hour at which her father had

Electra enters alone, for she is quintessentially alone in this hostile
world, and the reason that she has clasped so tenaciously and so long
to the memory of her beloved father immediately becomes obvious.
Agamemnon is the one being to whom she can turn, if only within the
recesses of her own tortured memory. He belongs to her if for no other
reason than by virtue of her loyalty and need of him. Strauss has here
psychologized the Greek theme of revenge and remembrance. Here,
the daughter clings to the memory of her beloved father as does any
lonely child in an oppressive and hostile environment.

The spirit of the dead king is not confined to any one area of the
stage. Unlike the Ghost of Hamlet who had been banished from his
own court, Agamemnon here lies in an undefined grave somewhere,
and consequently everywhere, beneath the flagstones of this outer
courtyard. This opera works along the psychological principles of
repression: it is because Agamemnon and his murder are so utterly
denied by the queen and the world of her servants that the dead king
becomes the most forceful and all-pervasive presence in the play. The
musical motif associated with Agamemnon thus represents the untram-
melable force of the repressed subconscious that threatens to overthrow
alike the individual and the state.

The tragic heroine enters at dusk, the hour at which her father had
been murdered so many years earlier. She laments his murder and calls
to him, as to her only ally, not to leave her languishing in this hostile
world but to appear to her as he had done the night before, by means
of his shadow passing along the wall. In this sense, the ghost of her dead
father constitutes Electra's very life-force. She lives for him alone. Here,
in place of the red light that Reinhardt had used to indicate the ghostly
presence of Agamemnon, Strauss has introduced a musical "Agamemnon" motif, one that together with the shadows, the desperate call of
Electra and the sense that this entire stage is in some way the burial-

ground of Agamemnon, introduces the presence of the murdered king and father as one that will be pervasive throughout. Electra is the only one to mention Agamemnon. It is she who keeps the spirit of her father alive and palpable in the courtyard in which he has been buried. It is because of Electra, the daughter, that the presence of the father permeates the play and propels the characters into action.

Electra is the guardian of the grave and spirit of her father. When in the recognition scene Orestes asks if she is "related in blood to them who died," Electra proudly declares: "Related? I?/ I *am* that blood!"[96] (emphasis added) and, as such, she is the priestess of the dead. Electra, the unmated, has dedicated her life to the spirit of her father in a way that a Christian nun dedicates herself to Christ. She is the virgin-priestess that we had met in Aeschylus' play and, as such, she is endowed with powers from the invisible gods. It is surely in recognition of this, Electra's particular role, that Clytemnestra approaches her daughter across the barrier of their mutual hatred as a suppliant for a cure against her nightmares.

Bales points out that in Strauss' opera, Clytemnestra and her two daughters are all victims of their own arrested psychological development. Chrysothemis comes to warn her sister that Aegisthus and the queen are planning to remove her forever from the light of day should she not curb her anger against them (a punishment that Chrysothemis herself, who so longs for life, could never tolerate), but Electra considers her sister a collaborator, the "daughter of your mother."[97] She greets Chrysothemis with the petulance of the adolescent, ordering her to deliver her message and remove herself from her sight. In a similar manner, that which ultimately destroys the one half-moment that Clytemnestra and Electra share is not Electra's poisonous memories and vindictiveness against her mother, but her being confronted again by her mother's infantile savagery and her realization that the queen is blinded by her egocentricity, by her childlike horror of her dreams and by her need to rid herself of them regardless of the suffering it might cause others. Bales claims that ultimately it is the queen's cruelly selfish cry:

> And must I let blood each beast that creeps and flies,
> and rise each day and sleep each night in the steam
> of their blood, like the race that lives in farthest Thule
> in bloodred mist: I will not dream again.

that thrusts Electra from her once again in hostility and rebuttal:

Your dreams will end when the right blood-sacrifice
falls beneath the axe.[98]

Electra is the moral conscience of a world that cruelly resembles
Europe at the turn of this century. She is symbiotically tied to her sister,
Chrysothemis, the principle of life, and, like a dead husk, she, the old
order, is shed at the end of the action in order to grant life to the
new.

Despite the psychological interpretation that Strauss gives his
opera and despite the expressionistic style that Reinhardt had used,
both artists remain true to the classic Greek form of the play. Are these
artists illustrating by means of this classic form in modern garb that the
passage of time is no guarantee of human progress? Are they dramatiz-
ing Freud's theory that violence is an integral part of man and of
Western civilization which for the sake of civilization has to be repressed, yet which by force of nature is bound periodically to erupt?[99]
Were these artists recognizing, within Electra's dance of death, the in-
evitability of war and devastation in Europe?

What has happened to ritual in this world in which there is no
longer any shared worldview and in which the spectators arrive for the
performance with a completely different approach to life and theater
than that of the performers? The emotional threat that this dramatization of wild, imprisoned women must have had upon its audience, the
savage outburst of instinctual violence that it depicts as the underlying
force that threatened to erupt and destroy the orderly world of 1909
Berlin, must have been devastating. The screams, the colors of blood
and of violence, the ghostly musical reminder of the spirit of an older,
better age together with the threat of revolution that bombarded the
audience behind the closed doors of the Berlin theater must surely have
bonded the audience, at least for the duration of the performance, as
if fellow travellers in a hijacked airplane, or coparticipants in any other
civil or natural disaster. For the duration of the performance all are
ensnared within the same traumatic eruption of the intellect and the
senses, all are jolted out of their protective cloak of complacence, and
all are forced to reevaluate their previous understanding of reality.
This, I believe, is the ritual of today's theater. It is the drawing together
of strangers in an enclosed space in such a way as to change their
awareness. The values that are dramatized here with such force are not
those of the general society. "Sanity," "heroism" and "the act of
theater" itself are utterly foreign in this space from the way they seem
in the familiar, outer world. And we cling to the elements of violence

within the theater as one does to the carriage of the fairground roller-coaster in the fervent hope that they will grant us a safe landing.

Eugene O'Neill:
Mourning Becomes Electra (1931)

Freud transformed human experience to the extent that since the publication of his theories it has become very difficult to perceive reality in pre–Freudian terms. The change of focus that he created, from the effect that the many have over the individual to that which the individual with his myriad emotions and complex psychic structure has over his society, very much influenced American art forms during the 20s and 30s. Thus, in O'Neill's play, the repression of the Electra-figure which even in Greek times had physical, sexual and emotional connotations has become an exposé of arrested sexual and emotional growth. The myth of death and rebirth has moved from the universal to the personal. Here the theme has become morbidly turned in upon a totally solipsistic Lavinia/Orin personality, one that is unable to move beyond the point of its own stifled development. In sharp contrast to early Greek society, which had encouraged the process of death and rebirth by means of ritual, this society, like this household, becomes itself the instrument of a death that can allow for no rebirth:

MANNON

... nothing was clear except that there'd always been some barrier between us—a wall hiding us from each other![100]

The individual is the mirror of his society which we are unable to see other than in the caricature-figures of the chorus of gossips and slanderers. In a tight-lipped New England town such as this that is characterized more by its closed doors and shuttered windows than by any sense of community, there can be no growth, no journey toward manhood or the heroic and, consequently, no future, only an excruciating longing that is always there and that can never be appeased:

BECKWITH

Oh, Shenandoah, I long to hear you
A-way, my rolling river
Oh, Shenandoah, I can't get near you
Way-ay, I'm bound away
Across the wide Missouri [688]

The play moves from the exterior to the interior of the house and outward on to the water, as the dramatic concentration moves from objective reality to the internal, psychological motivations of the individual and, finally, to the diseased, unconscious regions of the mind. In this way the structure and separate spaces of the play create the theme. The life-defying alienation that exists between the characters on stage and between the actors and audience is theatrically created in the structure and separate spaces of the play.

Mourning Becomes Electra is the expression of a stagnant society. The house which, in Giraudoux' play (as we shall see later), is torn between tears and laughter, is here a house of doom. The curse of the House of Atreus here becomes the repressively Puritanical outlook of the Mannon family:

MANNON

That's always been the Mannon's way of thinking. They went to the white meeting-house on Sabbaths and meditated on death. Life was a dying. Being born was starting to die. Death was being born [738].

We are told that white pillars from its pagan facade cast dark, prison-like shadows across the Puritan front of this house. Despite their denial, these people are ultimately prisoners of their passions. The face of the house with its shuttered windows forms a mask of death, as do the faces of Clytemnestra, Electra, and Orestes and is a theatrical representation of the repression of emotions, a "putting on a front" for the outer world and, at the same time, a diminution of the exterior in order to explore the seething emotions within.

Here the theme of incest is a theatrical imaging of a family and of individuals that are turned in upon themselves in a way that can only presage death. Orin is an abomination, a victim of the oppressive and, consequently, deadly aspect of what we had identified in the Greek world as the Great Mother. He has been reduced from hero to impotent child, not by his society as much as by the psychological forces within his family structure. In this way, "Fate" that had played so powerful a part in the Classical world has become the inescapably intertwined forces of hereditary factors and family relationships. The interior of the house, with its massive furniture and its family portraits on the walls, personifies on stage the enormous ancestral burden that these characters have to bear. They cower Ibsen-like beneath the portraits of their ancestors. In this way the ghosts of their fathers are seen and felt at all times and, as the Aeschylean ghost, they directly influence the fate of their household. True to the traditional portrayal of the myth, Mannon has survived the death and destruction of civil war only to be overcome by the fate within his own family.

The ancient question of Electra's insanity which, since the time of Sophocles, had begun to represent the vigor of the antirational and the opponent of the establishment, is here Lavinia's insistence on maintaining, at all costs, a facade of normalcy over a consciousness of increasingly violent and volcanic behavior. It is also the disintegration of a boy who is incestuously attached to his mother and who will therefore never experience the "heroic" break from the maternal that is necessary for his journey toward manhood. Insanity is no longer an affront to the body-politic but the cause of chaos and devastation to the individual human being. Fate has moved from the realm of the gods to the insurmountable forces within the human soul, and is represented as such in images on stage.

In this play as in *The Prodigal* (which we shall see later in this study) water symbolizes what Peter Brook has termed the "empty space" and Herbert Blau, "the conscious state." It is the space which constitutes the beginning — the silent moment, the drawing into — of any theatrical event and here it is specifically the meeting-place of the unconscious mind around which the performers and the audience are congregated. It is Aeschylus' burial mound, the sacred center of the ritual, which draws actors and audience magnetically together in a common focus of concentration. It is the space to which the growing adolescent withdraws before taking upon himself the heroic return and the subsequent heroic action. It is the spiritual center that has been covered over in *Hamlet* and which forces itself on the periphery of the Shakespearean mind and stage. But here, in *Mourning Becomes Electra*, all of this has become a quagmire of hatred and repressed sexual desire from which the protagonist can never emerge. Water is the unconscious, the place of seething passion, memory, fear, violence and murder. It is an element of the human makeup that we most try to avoid, yet which, upon this stage, we are forced to witness and assess directly.

The stagnant, Puritan society of this small New England town has so alienated its members from one another that the Mannon household has become totally turned in upon itself. It is knotted and gnarled by incestuous introversion until, like some horrendous sick beast, it attacks and devours its own flesh. In Greek terms it is the epitome of the destructive Earth Mother.

Hatred has become the only vehicle of expression. Lavinia has always been as we see her here with her frigid exterior desperately controlling an illicit sexuality. Her tragic fall had occurred before her birth, with her grandfather's construction of this house of hatred and vengeance. Her mordant cry for revenge is her desperate appeal for love in a house that disdains the simple expression of emotional needs. Christine has evolved from the terrible Earth Mother of pagan times, who had sacrificed her drone-like husband for the fertility of nature, to a product of the Christian domestic tradition who just "wants out," and plunges tragically from one human trap to another. For in this deadly locked society there is no new blood, no hope for new life, only the ghostly repetition of the same name and the same house and the same situation over and over again.

Orin is the last of this sick chain of being, and the end of the Orestean line. As such, he is the weakest link. We see him entrenched in his preconscious stage, incestuously tied to the figure of his mother-sister:

ORIN

If I had been he I would have done what he did! I would have loved her as he loved her—killed Father too—for her sake! [803].

For him there is no heroic voyage for there is no hope of manhood. The demise of the mother necessitates the death of the undifferentiated son:

ORIN

Do you remember me telling you how the faces of the men I killed came back and changed to Father's face and finally became my own? . . . Maybe I've committed suicide! [198].

Jean Giraudoux: *Electra* (1937)

In a world in which there are no absolutes, the ironic takes the place of the tragic and the tragic hero becomes the un-hero. The justice that Electra awaits as the culmination of her aspirations becomes a grotesque mirror of violence. Orestes, the avenging arm of his sister and, as such, the youth seeking that heroism which we have recognized so far as manhood, perpetrates the deed out of mindless indifference. Manhood, heroism and justice are re-examined in this play and are found suspect.

It is perhaps a sign of their innocence that the Greeks had experienced guilt only as the aftermath of evil. The modern world is not
so lucky. Jean Giraudoux' *Electra* is a satirical parody of the tragic
mode. Here the Eumenides do not appear after Orestes' murder of
Clytemnestra and Aegisthus. They walk in with him as he arrives on
stage, suggesting in an almost Elizabethan way that they accompany
him onto the stage of life. They are grotesque, nasty little girls who
swell visibly as he experiences the reality of his myth. This is an antiheroic play in an age of antiheroes. The human being is pursued
throughout life by guilt and by grotesque, ugly, irksome questions.

The Eumenides form the chorus of the play, introducing the
characters and the action. Above all, they introduce an alienating atmosphere, a feeling of foreboding and discomfort. These are the Furies
of the modern stage and of modern life.

The setting is the palace of Argos. Orestes has never before seen
such a sensitive building. The right side of the palace is built

GARDENER

... of stones from Gaul and sweats at certain
seasons that the people say the palace is
weeping. The left side is built of marble from
Argos which is flooded by sunlight even at night.[101]

The palace laughs and cries at the same time. It is a house which
is as neurotic and as divided against itself as are the lives of those it
shelters and as the opposing forces of a divided Europe. Giraudoux
develops his characters along Euripidean lines. Clytemnestra is not all
evil: she is a confused, middle-aged, unloved woman who appeals
desperately to her daughter for understanding. She wants to be accepted as a woman, but Electra sees her only as a mother.

As a daughter Electra can neither understand nor forgive
Clytemnestra's repugnance for Agamemnon. Neither can she understand or accept her mother's need or right to be loved. Electra, like her
Euripidean counterpart, is dangerously unbalanced. Her need for
revenge against her mother has been smoldering for seven years.
Ironically, unlike the Electra character of ancient Greece, this Electra
is ignorant of the real reasons for her hatred. She persuades herself that
it is because her mother had let Orestes fall as a baby. The fall is symbolic of his fall from royalty to anonymity in exile, but it is dealt with
on a personal level.

Clytemnestra claims that she had dropped Orestes while holding him at arm's length to protect him from a sharp pin that she was wearing. The pin perhaps represents the sting, the by now familiar adder within the maternal breast, symbol of the ambivalence that the mother has for her son and of the son's desire to draw close to the mother. Clytemnestra accuses Electra, in turn, both of pushing Orestes away from her out of hatred and of attempting to clutch him to her in an incestuous embrace. All of these conflicting emotions were probably true and all no doubt represented the feelings that Giraudoux, the French diplomat, witnessed and experienced in prewar Germany.

The theme of incest between brother and sister is developed here, not to demonstrate the emergence of the hero, and not as an enactment of the theme of fertility, of death and resurrection in nature as it had in the original, Aeschylean version, but as a powerfully satirical devaluation of the "heroic." For despite the neurotic ambivalence of Electra, the heroic in this play is not masculine action. Here the men live by means of compromise and political expediency, not by any commitment to Truth. Heroism is represented, rather, in the guise of female integrity, memory and insistence on abstract ideals, an insistence which is both insane and impossible to live with. Again the female is the uncompromising figure of Electra. Again the female is associated with madness and truth.

PRESIDENT

If criminals don't forget their sins, if the conquered don't forget their defeats, if there are curses, quarrels, hatreds, the fault is not with humanity's conscience, which always tends toward compromise and forgetfulness, it lies with ten or fifteen women who make trouble.

STRANGER

I agree with you. Those ten or fifteen women save the world from egoism.

PRESIDENT

They save it from happiness. I know Electra. Let's agree that she is what you say—justice, generosity, duty. But it's by justice, generosity, duty, and not by egoism and easy going ways, that the state, individuals, and the best families are ruined.

PRESIDENT

. . . Happiness is never the lot of implacable people. A happy family makes a surrender. A happy epoch demands unanimous capitulation [143].

Giraudoux regarded prewar France as a nation that, for the sake of happiness, was making a "unanimous capitulation," as one that was rapidly losing its moral fiber, as a people whose innate sense of justice, loyalty, and patriotism was being forfeited for economic security and modernism. Moral values were corroding; institutions were disintegrating. In short, Giraudoux believed that his country was selling out to Prussianism, to mechanization, power and money, and that ultimately, despite the enormous inconvenience, only France's involvement in World War II could set it back on a course of courage and moral stability. In 1940 he wrote, "This war, the worst of evils, must be made to serve a purpose: to act as the sluice-gates between a bygone era and a new age."[102]

As in the Greek plays on the same theme, Electra longs for Orestes. He alone is capable of arousing in her embittered soul any feeling of love. He reveals himself and she clasps him to her in the archetypal embrace of the sister-lover. She has been the captive. He is to be her redeemer.

Perhaps as an extension of the Euripidean suggestion, Electra and Orestes here sleep together in total mutual symbiosis. This sleep is, again, the *hieros gamos*—the sacred marriage and the longed-for fusion of the oppositions within a hitherto fragmented mind as within a divided Europe. The *hieros gamos* is the perfect coming together and should give birth to the ideal human being, the ideal action or, perhaps, the ideal nation. Yet Electra will settle for nothing short of Justice as her ideal. Ironically, justice is achieved, but wears the mask of evil. The ideal action might be the restoration of justice, but to what extent is one able in the twentieth-century to perpetrate such a horrendous act, and maintain one's humanity? The perfect union represents the self-fulfillment that the hero wins after his greatest of struggles. As had been remarked earlier, it brings to mind the sacred marriage of Faust's Helen and Paris (Goethe) which, had it not been disrupted, would have produced the highest form of the alchemical ideal, a golden child. But Giraudoux' scene is played backward. The sacred marriage takes place *before* Orestes murders his mother and, instead of giving birth to a golden child, it produces in Electra a knowledge and memory of her mother's crime against her father, that is, an image of horror, an image of the *imperfect*. Thus, with extreme irony, it is Electra's uncompromising insistence on Justice that gives birth to the horrors of war.

As with Euripides, Giraudoux' Agamemnon had wanted to marry

Electra to a commoner (the gardener) because, as the beggar realizes, he is frightened that "one day she will become Electra." "She will begin to bite, to turn the city upside down, to push up the price of butter, start a war" (150).

Electra becomes Electra. That is, she grows from the neurotically hateful girl into the avenging fury during that one night of sacred union with her newfound brother-deliverer. Instead of producing hope for the future, this union has teased monsters from the past.

Electra stands for the absolute. As her name implies, she is extreme. She has the potential for light and clarity but she is by nature violent and uncompromising. It is as though she has been channeled through the deeds of her mother (earth, Physis and Remembrance) to burst with ruthless clarity upon mankind. Aegisthus recognizes the seer in Electra

> I knew I'd find her looking toward me, her statuesque head, her eyes which see only when the lids are closed, deaf to human speech [186].

For the world that Electra lives in is one of compromise. In this play, Electra is an anachronism. In an age of humanitarianism, she is the visionary who cannot see humanity. If there is a Chrysothemis in this play, it is Agatha, the mindless, childlike bride of the President of the Council, a woman who marries for status and protection and loves for the satisfaction of her sexual appetites. All the characters are sadly ordinary, but their petty greed, their lust and their hunger for love are less threatening than the heroic. Aegisthus says

> If for ten years the gods have not meddled with our lives it is because I kept the heights empty and the fairground full ... our poor neighboring cities betray themselves by erecting their gallows on the top of a hill. I crucify at the bottom of a valley [148].

Safety lies in anonymity, in not tempting fate. Here there is no heroic struggle and no transformation into manhood. Orestes, the avenging hero, is not roused to passion by means of any communal incantations or libations to the gods as in Aeschylus. He is not a man of action, craft and noble purpose as in Sophocles, nor is he a man torn between filial love and duty as in Euripides. He is merely a soft-spoken stranger, with no particular commitment but with a nostalgia for his hometown and a feeling of affection for his sister. There is no passion in his matricide and murder. It is merely the logical consequence of Electra's inquisition. It is the unheroic deed of the unhero, the undifferentiated youth.

The nearest we come to a masculine form of heroism, within
Giraudoux' *Electra*, is in the practical leadership ability that suddenly
develops at the end of the action within the character of Aegisthus, the
repressive figure of masculine authority:

AEGISTHUS

Electra, you're in my power. Your brother too. I can kill you. Yesterday I should have killed you. Instead of that I promise as soon as the
enemy is repulsed, to step down from the throne and place Orestes
on it.

. . . Tomorrow, before the altar where we celebrate our victory the
guilty man shall stand, for there is only one guilty man in a parricide's
coat. He'll confess his crime publicly and determine his punishment
himself. First let me save the city [198].

In the low "fair-ground" of our un-classical reality, it is not "the
purest, the handsomest, the youngest" HERO, in whom Electra
places her trust, that saves the city [191].

If there is any idealization in this play, it is that of the practical
man-of-action, the rational politician who does not allow himself to be
swayed by passion, and of the common sinner with potential for good:

AESISTHUS

Do you doubt my sincerity?

ELECTRA

I don't doubt it. I recognize in it the hypocrisy and malice of the gods.
They change a parasite into a just man, an adulterer into a husband,
a usurper into a king. They thought my task not painful enough, so
they made a figure of honor out of you, whom I despise! [192].

This is the opposite of the "heroic" so admired by the Greeks.

The beggar foresees that Electra will reveal herself as Electra and
that the king will "reveal himself as Aegisthus." At the moment that
Electra emerges as the avenger of objective truth and universal justice,
the king grows from a petty tyrant to a man capable of delivering the
city into peace. Truth has emerged as an abstraction, an ideal that is
antithetical to peace, and Aegisthus begs Electra to delay her truth for
the sake of his city. But "the beautiful and cruel thing about truth is
that she is eternal, but is also like a flash of lightning" (196) — such is
the nature of Electra. Aegisthus, the harbinger of peace, has blood on
his hands and he placates the crowd with half-truths pretending he is

already married to Clytemnestra. Electra, the voice of the absolute, cannot brook such compromise. For her, peace can come only after the total eradication of the present order. Despite the deliberately anti-classical, episodic structure of the play, Electra's tunnel vision reveals itself to us within the traditional form of the tragic heroine. Her moral vision is contradictory to our own.

The nasty little Furies have grown to the stature of Electra. They are Electra. As such they will leave Argos and hound Orestes who, far from being the newly matured youth on his heroic journey to manhood, is merely an innocent vehicle of death.

SEC. FURY

Satisfied Electra? The city . . . is dying.

ELECTRA

I am satisfied. I know that it will be born again.

For the tragic heroine who knows only extremes, life can be resumed only after total destruction:

THIRD FURY

And the people killing each other in the streets will they be born again?

ELECTRA

I have my conscience. I have Orestes. I have justice. I have everything [203].

Electra, the ruthless voice of Physis and remembrance, has a morality that is true only to herself.

The Olympian vision of the relentless and unalterable cosmic order and the need that Greek tragedy had to bring man into harmony with the forces of nature have no place in the modern world. Giraudoux has untied the knot that has bound man to heroism. The lofty but willful gods of the Greeks are reduced to a meddlesome beggar who sits, essentially off centerstage, observing the sufferings of his fellow characters with callous objectivity, and a pathetic band of outcasts who come as a *Deus ex Machina* to deliver Orestes and Electra not from murder, but for murder. The tragedy wends its way from episode to episode with no regard for character plausibility, tragic flaws, recognition or reversals. All aspects of Aristotelian tragedy are somehow suggested but missed. We are familiar with the Aristotelian necessity that the tragic hero fall from a lofty and admired position and with the fact that only the particular circumstances of a hero's life make him or her commit the tragic deed. Yet Electra lives on in the palace of her dead father and she remains throughout Electra, that fiery element that wields clarity and destruction and accepts no compromise.

The heroic is in question and tragedy, the heroic form, has fallen. Aegisthus challenges Electra's classical justice

> And you dare call this justice, that makes you burn your city, damn your family; you dare call this the justice of the gods?

and Electra replies:

> . . . There are criminals we love, murderers we embrace. But when the crime is an assault on human dignity, infects a nation, corrupts its loyalty, then—no pardon is possible [195].

Electra is condemned for her extremism. Yet how would we respond today? How would this apply, for example, to the election of Kurt Waldheim as chancellor of Austria? What if Giraudoux had written this play a few years later, after World War II? Would the supreme moral voice of Physis not seem more plausible?

Giraudoux' use of irony is his means of creating in physical form the ambiguity of the writer, the era, the audience and morality in general, as well as the ambiguity that bourgeois audiences have towards their own ideals. It is by means of the poet's use of images, of the sensual, of passion and empathy that he stimulates the humanity of the spectators. David Cole writes, "[We] recognize the images which the theatre depends upon our recognizing because to be human is to recognize them."[104] Again theater has become the raising of issues between players and spectators in such a way as to form a focal point of attention. Those reactions which are provoked on a particular stage at a particular moment as the direct result of all the combined elements of the performance, form a bond which constitutes the theatrical event.

Robinson Jeffers:
The Tower Beyond Tragedy (1937)

Robinson Jeffers was born in Pittsburgh, Pennsylvania, of Anglo-Irish parents on January 10, 1887, but moved to the West Coast with his family while still quite young. He has been described as an individualist, as somewhat of a recluse, as gentle, reserved and meditative. He was raised in a strict, Calvinist home and educated by his father in the classics. On August 2, 1913, he married Una Cull, an extremely beautiful and well-educated woman with whom he had been in love for several years. The young couple intended to settle in England but were forced because of the outbreak of World War I to make Northern California their home. Jeffers wrote:

> ... the August news turned us to this village of Carmel instead; and when the stage-coach topped the hill from Monterey, and we looked down through pines and sea-fogs on Carmel Bay, it was evident that we had come without knowing it to our inevitable place.[105]

It was in the isolation of these mountains that Jeffers found his true purpose. He loved the mists, the sunsets, the low clouds and the mystical wildness of the ocean. For five years, this solitary, introverted man became a landmark for passers-by who saw him daily extracting massive boulders out of the rocks of the shoreline and lugging them to his home on a kind of primitive pulley that is believed to have been used by ancient Egyptians in the construction of their Sphinx. The erection of his tower, which became famous as Tor House, afforded Jeffers a profound sense of peace and when it was completed, he would climb at nightfall to its summit and meditate. He described the scenery around his home in the following way:

> The Santa Lucian hills overlook the Carmel River and extend southward along the coast. The northernmost slopes are pine-crested; the valleys beyond are forested with redwoods (sequoias) and oaks and Santa Luciian firs. This region, and the peninsula, are made aerially beautiful by cloud-play and the frequent ocean-mists. The clouds most often hang long, half veiling the hills; yet the atmosphere is singularly transparent, and I have been astonished by the brilliancy of the sky during thunderstorms, in heavy and starless nights.[106]

Perhaps during the war years this view atop the human landscape afforded the poet his own private "tower beyond tragedy."

In an interview, Una Jeffers talked with Lawrence Clark Powell about the ambivalence her husband had had regarding America's involvement in the war. "He disliked the cant of neutrality, followed by the cant of our belligerency." She said that he had been torn between a feeling of obligation to enlist in the military forces and his obligation to stay in Carmel and support his young family. She elaborated:

The conflict of motives on the subject of going to war or not was probably one of several factors that, about this time, made the world and his own mind much more real and intense to him. Another factor was the building of Tor House. As he helped the masons shift and place the wind and wave-worn granite I think he realized some kinship with it, and became aware of strengths in himself unknown before. Thus at the age of thirty-one there came to him a kind of *awakening such as adolescents and religious converts are said to experience.*[107]

Louis Adamic was a close friend and biographer of Jeffers. He wrote:

The human breed is degenerating (no doubt about it and no way to stop the process) and, viewing it in the mirror of his own mind, his cosmic consciousness, and in relation to the universe, he finds it offensive. America is a "perishing Republic" and will have "centuries of increasing decadence." There is a limited sort of salvation only for the individual. One can crawl into his cave and stay there. A heron a-wing "over the black ebb" is dearer to him than the "many pieces of humanity . . . gathering shellfish" and dropping "paper and other filth" on his beach, heedless of the sign warning them against it which he has stuck by the road that winds through his place. Indeed, "humanity is needless." . . . He warns his young boys to be moderate in their "love of man" and goes on singing of points Lobos and Sur, of his own hopelessness and violence, . . . of the elements in their dramatic moods, of Time and Space.[108]

One cannot help regarding the elitist isolationism of this American poet as a rare luxury. No doubt many in Europe at this time would also have relished the opportunity to escape the ravages of war.

The "awakening" that Una had attributed to her husband bears an uncanny similarity to the one that we have observed so far as having been experienced alike by the prophet, the maturing adolescent, and the hero on their return from their own isolation. It is the awakening that constitutes in particular the starting point of the Electra plays, and perhaps, in general, that of the tragic form.

Jeffers bases his song of matricide, incest and madness upon the already familiar context of the Electra myth. From the perspective of the twentieth century, the myth itself has become as timeless as the eternally recurring cycle of passion and violence that it depicts. In it, the characters are fated to an endless chain of emotional torture for they are deprived of any psychological and emotional movement other than that allotted to them within the perimeters of the theme that has typified their story so far. The larger than life characters within this dramatic poem are spun of a human intensity that can never be

disentangled within the context of the myth. In a Levi-Straussian
understanding of tragedy they suffer from being too close to one
another:

ORESTES

... I saw a vision of us move in the dark:
all that we did or dreamed of
Regarded each other, the man persued the
    woman, the woman clung to the man, warriors and
    kings
Strained at each other in the darkness, all loved
    or fought inward, each one of the lost people
Sought the eyes of another that another should
    praise him; sought never his own but another's;
    the net of desire
Had every nerve drawn to the center, so that they
    writhed like a full draught of fishes, all matted
In the one mesh...
It is all turned inward, all your desires
    incestuous, the woman the serpent, the man the
    rose-red cavern
Both human, worship forever...[109]

In this context the theme of incest becomes emblematic of the
introverted and convoluted relationships that suffocate the hero and
prevent him from realizing the potential of the greater world of which
he is a part. In this context, also, the hero becomes he who can liberate
himself from the suffocation of emotional, social and political ties.
Orestes is such a hero:

ORESTES

...
As for me, I have slain my mother.
...
And the gate's open,
    the gray boils over the mountain, I have greater
kindred than dwell under a roof...
... I have cut the meshes
And fly like a freed falcon [138].

Jeffers' medium is poetry, language of myth, passion and madness. With her own naked body, in the ultimate act of sexual antago-
nism, Clytemnestra masters and holds at bay the savage, hungry
men-of-war that surround her. The queen, a figure of hypnotic, mythic
stature, manipulates ritual in a desperate attempt to control her

environment and to transform her murderous ecstasy into order and acceptance.

CLYTEMNESTRA

I rule you, I.
The Gods have satisfied themselves in this man's
    death; there shall not one drop of the blood of
    the city
Be shed further. I say the high Gods are content;
    as for the lower,
And the great ghost of the King: my slaves will
    bring out the King's body decently before you
And set it here, in the eyes of the city: spices
    the ships bring from the south will comfort his
    spirit;
    Mycenae and Tiryns and the shores will mourn him
    aloud; sheep will be slain for him; a hundred
    beeves
Spill their thick blood into the trenches;
    captives and slaves go down to serve him, yes all
    these captives
Burn in the ten-day fire with him, unmeasured wine
    quench it, urned in pure gold the gathered ashes
Rest forever in the sacred rock; honored; a
    conqueror...
    ...
A woman among lions! Ah, the King's power, ah the
    King's victories! Weep for me, Mycenae!
Widowed of the King! [97–8].

Agamemnon's death has turned into a veritable feast of the gods who, as Clytemnestra later says, "love what men call crime" (110). There is a distinct hierarchy here between the indifferent gods, the beautifully white-skinned and treacherous aristocracy, and those "dogs," the common men with their "poor brown and spotted women" (107) who serve as fodder for the appetites of their masters. The Greek plays had been aristocratic, not only in tone, but also by virtue of the enormous distance that had existed between the lives of the aristocracy and those of the peasants. In this modern work there is a sinister closeness between the victims and the victimizers of society. As with Hofmannsthal's play there is a sense of the relentless perpetuity of human suffering, specifically the suffering of the masses, the "slaves," at the hands of those that are in power. In an interesting reinterpretation of the theme of ritual as the play of death and rebirth, the slaves must go

down with the assassinated ruler to guarantee the life and security of
the vanquishing head of state.

In *Violence and the Sacred*, René Girard describes the sacrificial
rites of primitive communities, much as Freud does in *Totem and
Taboo*, as a communal experience within which all participants are
united in a blood-bond with the sacrificial victim. He maintains that
communities, in their effort to establish a lasting civilization, held to
rigid laws of status and position, that so long as everyone adhered to
his or her rank in society things ran smoothly, but as soon as one
member was dislodged from his or her appointed status the rest of the
social pyramid began to crumble. Girard writes:

> The sacrificial crisis can be defined, therefore, as a crisis of distinc-
> tions—that is, a crisis affecting the cultural order. This cultural order
> is nothing more than a regulated system of distinctions in which the
> differences among individuals are used to establish their "identity"
> and their mutual relationships.

He claims that

> When the religious framework of a society starts to totter, it is not ex-
> clusively or immediately the physical security of the society that is
> threatened; rather, the whole cultural foundation of the society is put
> in jeopardy. The institutions lose their vitality; the protective facade
> of the society gives way; social values are rapidly eroded, and the
> whole cultural structure seems on the verge of collapse.
>
>   A single principle is at work in primitive religion and classical
> tragedy alike, a principle implicit but fundamental. Order, peace,
> and fecundity depend on cultural distinctions; it is not these distinc-
> tions but the loss of them that gives birth to fierce rivalries and sets
> members of the same family or social group at one another's
> throats.[113]

According to Girard, such a society under threat of disintegration
needed to sidetrack its destructive attention and intentions from
members of its own community and project its hostility onto some objective scapegoat. Only in such a way could all the members of the community regroup harmoniously within a collective hostility against one
common enemy. With a clear-eyed scrutiny of that kind of victimization which has characterized Western civilization from the time of
Oedipus and Electra to the twentieth century, Girard claims that

> When a community succeeds in convincing itself that one alone of
> its number is responsible for the violent mimesis besetting it; when
> it is able to view this member as the single "polluted" enemy who

is contaminating the rest; and when the citizens are truly unanimous in this conviction—then the belief becomes a reality, for there will no longer exist elsewhere in the community a form of violence to be followed or opposed.

Girard defines such an "enemy" as the sacrificial victim, as one who has to be of sufficient stature to attract the attention of the entire community. Regicide is the most extreme example of the corrosion of state-hierarchy, yet here in an act of will that surpasses that of the gods themselves Clytemnestra transforms the king into the sacrificial offering and forces the community of savage men into a ritual of obeisance and reorientation.

In this drama the knot of ambition, passion, love and hatred draws increasingly in upon itself in an ever tighter hold of desire and incest to a point of total narcissism. If there are any Eumenides in this poem, elements of the "feminine" that are at once a blessing and a curse, we might recognize them in the passion with which Electra attempts to hold her brother, and which represents the cloying, parasitical, human need that she has of him. Just as the repeated crimes of passion within the trilogy of Aeschylus had ended with a break from primal law for the more objective space of public order, so Jeffers frees his hero from the blood knot of human relationships for the emancipation of the individual mind. Orestes, the insane adolescent, breaks from the lure of the sister-lover and wanders alone in a "cloud upon the feasting gods, lightning and madness" (107). Again, this myth becomes the drama of the adolescent's liberation from primal ties as represented by the passions. Again, the hero reaches ultimately for the lone and dangerous regions of the spirit.

This Orestes is a hero, not an Aeschylean representative of the community of spectators, nor even the reluctant bearer of the human burden (as we will see in Sartre), but he who can free himself from the fetters, from the suffocation and the myopia, of social demands and emotional ties. With sharp psychological insight, the modern poet has lifted the dramatic screens of "Justice," "Vengeance" and "Heroism" and discovered a frighteningly personal, authentic motive for matricide, the most heinous of human crimes.

For here the hero's murder of his mother is not an act of revenge but of personal emancipation by means of which Orestes and perhaps Jeffers the poet liberate themselves imaginatively from their bondage to physical, domestic and political ties for the broader regions of the spiritual and the poetic that are associated with inspiration and madness and which represent here the ultimate human goal. It would seem that in his *Tower Beyond Tragedy* the poet has come full circle to the amoral, Homeric idealization of heroic man and his personal pursuit of excellence, yet, because social intercourse is regarded by him as violent and destructive, the poet's isolationist stance here becomes the one remaining moral alternative in an otherwise immoral world.

Perhaps the most obvious difference between Aeschylus' play and the poem by Jeffers is that in the former, Electra is unable to mask her true emotions. In the earlier play, Electra is escorted and encouraged by her chorus of women attendants, while in the latter she returns to Mycenae as a silent, scheming beggar-girl in pathetic isolation. Her filthy, ragged clothes represent the ugliness of her situation: a girl of such tender age, yet of such murderous hatred and able to dissemble with such finesse.

Both the destructive dependence that seems to typify human relationships in this play and that so impedes individual freedom, and the readiness of both mother and daughter to use their sexual favors as barter are the result of the cruelty of a society that is not mutually-supportive, but which rather preys upon its members. They are the result of a violence that tears the individual from his or her sense of self and place in the larger scheme of things, and fills him or her, like some besieged citadel, with the single and desperate need to dissemble, to attack and to defend. This, then, is Jeffers' ironic vision of the singleness of purpose that we had identified, in the earlier versions of the myth, as characteristic of the tragic heroine. The ritual of communion that had typified the world and the theater of ancient Greece and which had provided the protagonists with a sense of belonging is transformed within Jeffers' play into the cloying neediness of human relationships. It is a perverse, cruel closeness that forces the hero into flight.

As in the Hofmannsthal version, this violent world is a world of women. Clytemnestra is virulent and powerful as murderess, ruler and lover. She has the full force of Aeschylus' demonic heroine and the same measure of justification for her act, but she also has the sad realism of the twentieth century:

ORESTES

... This, a God in his temple
Openly commanded.

CLYTEMNESTRA

Ah, child, child, who has mistaught you and who has
          betrayed you? What voice has the God?
How was it different from a man's and did you see him?
Who sent the priest presents? They fool us,
And the Gods let them [125].

And the tragic, intuitive knowledge of the psychological torment that
violence will cause:

CLYTEMNESTRA

. . . this much I pray, for your sake, not
     with your hand, not with your hand, or
     the memory
Will so mother you, so glue to you, so
     embracing you,
Not the deep sea's green day, no cleft
     of a rock in the bed of the deep sea,
     no ocean of darkness
Outside the stars, will hide nor wash
     you [125].

What she does not know is that this hero is capable of freeing himself
once and for all from the emotional trap of mother and sister, from the
emotional trap of the myth itself by simply walking away.

As in the Hofmannsthal version of the myth, Electra is here the
prime schemer and motivator who goads a reluctant lad into an act of
murder. Unlike the Sophocles version, in which it was Orestes, the
hero, that had epitomized cunning and action, it is Jeffers' Electra who
warns:

. . . Brother though the great house is silent hark the
city [126].

Cassandra, the final female character around whom this poem was
built, provides the dramatic function of the chorus and is the spiritual
medium through which the, by now, familiar patriarchal judgment is
heard:

THE BODY OF CASSANDRA

I say if you let this woman live, this crime
go unpunished, what man among you
Will be safe in his bed? The woman ever envies
the man, his strength, his freedom, his loves.

> Her envy is like a snake beside him, all his life
>   through, her envy and hatred: law tames that
>   viper:
> Law dies if the Queen die not: the viper is free
>   then [100].

It is the expression of the male fear of female entrapment that had been so dramatically brought home to us in Clytemnestra's first scene: the brazen manner in which, with her naked body, she had taunted and defied the surrounding host of hostile men, and it is the suggestion that patriarchal law has been instigated for the specific end of emancipating man from her strangulating, emotional and sexual hold. The audience recognizes the masculine need to master the female again when the spirit of the murdered king violently takes possession of the body of Cassandra and, by so doing, forces her into the expression of his will:

BODY OF CASSANDRA

>   and having tasted
> The toad that serves women for heart. From now on may
> all bridegrooms
> Marry them with swords. Those that have borne
>   children
> Their sons rape them with spears [106–7].

Cassandra stands on the steps of the city, stalwart guardian of Agamemnon's place of murder and watchdog of the future. She is the medium through which the mighty powers of European history flow, a history of repeated acts of acquisition, violence and destruction:

CASSANDRA

> Curse Athens for the joy and the marble, curse
>   Corinth
> For the wine and the purple, and Syracuse
> For the gold and the ships; but Rome, Rome,
> With many destructions for the corn and the laws
>   and the javelins, the insolence, the threefold
> Abominable power: pass the humble
> And the lordships of darkness, but far down
> Smite Spain for the blood on the sunset gold,
>   curse France
> For the fields abounding and the running rivers,
>   the lights in the cities, the laughter, curse
>   England

For the meat on the tables and the terrible gray
　　ships, for old laws, far dominions, there remains
A mightier to be cursed and a higher for
　　malediction
When America has eaten Europe and takes tribute of
　　Asia, when the ends of the world grow aware of
　　each other
And are dogs in one kennel, they will tear
The master of the hunt with the mouths of the
　　pack: new fallings, new risings, O winged one
No end of the fallings and risings? An end shall
　　be surely,
Though unnatural things are accomplished, they
　　breathe in the sea's depth,
They swim in the air, they bridle the cloud-leaper
　　lightning to carry their messages [114].

It is an endless account of the suffering and violence of humanity:

CASSANDRA

Make me air to wander free between the stars and
　　the peaks; but cut humanity
Out of my being, that is the wound that festers in
　　me [115].

The years flow through Cassandra's unflinching body until Orestes and Electra return to complete the cycle of murder and revenge:

CASSANDRA

. . . Eight years I have seen the phantoms
Walk up and down this stair; and the rocks groan
　　in the night, . . .
　　. . .
. . . I am not Cassandra
But a counter of sunrises, permitted to live
　　because I am crying to die [116].

　　Jeffers' choice of language and dramatic structure reinforces his theme of idealized distancing. His dramatic poem is set in the mythical past; his poetic form is itself a kind of alienation and the highly ritualistic style of his drama produces the opposite effect to that which the ritual of community had upon Aeschylus' audience, for ritual in the 1930s deliberately separates the actors from their community, allowing each of the spectators to embark upon a separate imaginative voyage to a personal and individual source of inspiration and consequent reflection.

VI

The further the essentially male "hero" is brought into the war-ravaged world of the 20th century the further removed he becomes from his original "heroic" persona, the less masculine become his characteristics, and the weaker become his ties with the establishment: with tradition and with history; with community as well as with the precepts of church and state; with the particular ideology of his "personal" and also with those of his "collective" father. In this new antihero we recognize a representative spirit, one that questions — alone — a world into which he has been thrust and which is not of his making.

World War II plunged Western culture into an open-eyed acknowledgment of its own appetite for evil. The shrunken world of today's mass media is daily bombarded by the reaffirmation of its own violence. Where does the hero go from here? What effect does his knowledge of history, education and religion have on his actions? No longer can today's antihero find safe haven in the sanctuary of humankind. Each stands naked and terrified before the responsibility of his actions.

Jean-Paul Sartre: *Les Mouches* (1942)

Sartre was mobilized into the French Forces in 1939 and taken prisoner in 1940. He played an active part in the French Resistance and devoted many years after the war to questions of patriotism, loyalty, commitment and personal freedom, all of which are issues that we have encountered repeatedly within the myth of Electra. *Les Mouches* was written in 1942 under German Occupation.

It is appropriate, therefore, for Sartre to have chosen the figures of Electra and Orestes to question, yet again, the archetypal issues of lack of freedom, vengeance, collaboration, violence and the tainted soul, this time under the occupation of Vichy, France. In this play, Sartre presents us with a chorus of collaborators in the background figures of the citizens of Argos — men and women who are eternally imprisoned in Christian guilt — and with the innocent Electra crying for vengeance. Yet Sartre questions whether this Electra can handle that vengeance. More even than Sophocles' heroine, the female principle within Sartre's hero becomes the unheroic, eternally impotent voice of Physis. Only the totally emancipated "masculine" soul, that is, he or she who is conscious of his or her freedom from the "feminine" qualities of religion, superstition and the grip that history has always had upon the individual, only the hero that is free from the legacy of Agamemnon, can handle the burden of vengeance. The individual is not determined by any larger destiny, but has — consciously — to forge his or her own path. Again we see a kinship between the modern hero and his or her pre–Sophoclean counterpart, the amoral Homeric *arete* hero. Sartre's Orestes is the hero of the twentieth century. His emergence, as such, necessitates the shattering and shedding of the Christian soul, the emotional, female part of him as represented by Electra. Heroism of the war years demands clear-eyed action, not emotion.

Once again it is important for us to keep in mind that the hero has always been depicted in masculine form. My insistence, here, on broadening the general definition of "hero" to include the female, might well be a mistake. We might discover that women, whose development has been neither sufficiently understood nor recorded, might not have the personality structure, the drives or the appetites to fit the "heroic," as it has been defined up until our own moment in history. I leave it to the reader to question.

Sartre's Orestes is no longer essentially a member of a community. He has no necessary affiliation to the gods, to God, or to his own human lineage. As enlightened human being, he is free of all the superstitious ties with which history has entangled him, yet he is alone and desperately lonely in his freedom. The choice which will determine his subsequent actions is his to make; it is his choice also either to identify with his sister and the people of his hometown, or, with impunity, to turn his back on them. Ultimately, Orestes chooses commitment, not out of any moral obligation, but out of a need to belong. His identification is therefore ironically emotional, not heroic. Those who stood as silent witnesses of the Nazi occupation of France in effect chose acquiescence; that is, they took a stand that defined their lives thereafter as accomplices to murder.

Orestes takes a stand against murder in order to free himself of the solitude and the emptiness of his own religious emancipation. We might regard this as the opposite stand to the one which was taken by Jeffers' hero. His choice is fortuitously, but not essentially, a moral one.

Morality as an abstraction has no place here. His choice is made intelligently, guiltlessly and free of superstition, for he is free from the burden of history. Yet, again with an ironic twist, from the moment that he makes his commitment he becomes a part of history with all the emotional baggage that that entails. He has the comfort, but also the heavy, social burden (the flies), of belonging. He has chosen to be rooted in society and, by so doing, he has defined himself and his existence. He has taken upon himself the pain of human history. As such, despite himself, Sartre's Orestes assumes the status of the emerging hero.

Almost in the manner of the allegorical Pied-Piper, Orestes arrives from a guiltless, outer region, draws upon himself the unbearable burden (flies) of this city and leaves, hounded from that time onward by the implications of his action. The part that this character has just played before his spectators has bound him to them in a ritual of murder that is a precursor of personal sacrifice but renewed communal life. In Sartre's play it is not the gods that propel the hero into action, but the conscious choice of the private citizen.

Here again, Peter Brook's "empty space,"[114] the "conscious state," "freedom" itself lie beyond the perimeters of the stage. Orestes brings with him from offstage a climate of spiritual emancipation both to the players and to the audience. Again, both players and spectators are caught up within the theatrical event, within this ritual reenactment of the issues of commitment versus freedom, patriotism, personal conscience, "heroic" action, murder and the renewal of life. Brechtian reflection on the part of the spectators grows directly out of the action. Nothing is brought to the theatrical experience other than the innate conflicts within the human soul. Electra, Orestes and the citizens of Argos are the agons of a moral dilemma that has surfaced under Nazi occupation. They are the invisible made visible. They provoke thought and questioning. They are live theater.

Ezra Pound: *Elektra* (1951)

Ezra Pound's adaptation of the Sophoclean *Electra* was produced in 1987 under the artistic directorship of Carey Perloff at the Classic Stage Company Repertory Theater on East 13th Street, New York.

Pound had become convinced that "Usura" or "credit capitalism" lay at the root of the evils of society and he integrated this conviction into his own anti–Semitic, pro–Fascist ideology. During the war he gave a series of pro–Fascist broadcasts over the Rome radio service for which he was charged with treason by the American Military Government in 1945.

As a result of his plea of insanity, Pound escaped the death sentence and was incarcerated in Washington for thirteen years at the St. Elizabeth's Hospital for the criminally insane. It was in this setting in 1949 that Pound began his interpretation of Sophocles' *Electra* with the collaboration of Rudd Fleming, at that time a faculty member at the University of Maryland. The work was completed in 1951 but was never published, for fear, it is believed, that it would prove the author's sanity.

Pound was notorious for his aggressive use of rhythm and for the way in which he combined formal and colloquial language styles. Carey Perloff claims:

> In Pound's world there is no separation between past and present: as long as the poet can travel there, all times are present. Nor is there separation of languages: Pound took hold of the chiselled, precise, highly rhythmic language of ancient Greece with both hands and planted it firmly in Twentieth Century America.[115]

We have identified the Electra theme as the confrontation of the old by the herald of the new and, as such, *Electra* is a particularly suitable theme for this poet. In addition, although Fleming claims that Pound never specifically mentioned any personal reasons for his manipulation of this theme, it seems most likely that he recognized the similarity, both between the devastation of postwar Europe and that of ancient Greece, and that of his own situation with that of the Classical Greek heroine: both are incarcerated, both rage against the injustice of their plight and both await their liberation from impending insanity and death.

Pound's language vacillates drastically between the classical and the lyrical of the majestic heroine and rough, inner-city colloquialisms that reflect the naked squalor of a young girl who is trapped, rejected and maligned. Electra is isolated from the other characters within the poetry of her language and her tragic situation. She, alone, speaks in poetic form.

Pound's play becomes somewhat of a diatribe against the European forces for having sacrificed their sons, their greatest hopes, to war:

ELECTRA

All that is left me
my hope was Orestes
dust is returned me
in my hands nothing, dust that is all of him'
flower that went forth
. . .

Far from thy homeland
died far in exile
no hand was near thee
to soothe thy passing,
corpse unannointed
fire consumed thee,
all now is nothing'
strangers have brought thee
small in this urn here
sorrow upon me
fruitless my caring.[116]

And

It's the end of the line
we're all there together
ashes [71].

He seems to regard the past war and the present devastation, not
as the victory of Good over Evil, but more as the destructive, nihilistic
force of history itself and, by so doing, he transforms the death-wish
of the Greek heroine, her desperate need to be buried alive with the
ashes of her brother, into a modern postwar image of destruction:

ELECTRA

Dead Agamemnon, dead now my brother,
I am dead also, the great wind in passing
    bears us together,
Mirth for our foeman [73].

To Pound, the enormous heroic potential of the Orestean youth
has been reduced to a handful of ashes. The poet even seems to doubt
his nation's ability to recognize the significance of the European
destruction:

ORESTES

. . .all that is left of him
is this little jug, as you can see if you want to [70].

Thus, with horrendous irony the urn that had represented the fountainhead of spiritual inspiration and the centering force for community ritual has here been reduced to an image of loss and devastation. The dead of our own time hold no momentous significance, for they have no souls with which to possess us. Death here merely signifies emptiness and ashes. There is, however, an interesting twist to the theme of death and rebirth in the idealization of the revolutionary that seems to emerge. In this Poundian rendition of the myth, contrary to that of the Sophoclean hero, the life and vitality of the twentieth century lie in the hands of him who is willing to counter the power of the Establishment with his own daring. Orestes walks onto this stage with the readiness, the bluntness and the sensitivity of the proverbial rough diamond and, by so doing, his character stands in the same dramatic opposition to that of Electra as did his Sophoclean counterpart:

ELECTRA

Don't defraud me
of the pleasure of seeing you here

ORESTES

Damn well let anybody else try it. ... [84-5].

ELECTRA

Oh dearest friends
if now's to ear
a voice I ne'er
had hoped to hear
if joy shall not
burst forth at this
then ever dumb in wretchedness
should one live on in deep distress.
Now thou art here
in full daylight
shall I not pour
forth my delight,
who ne'er in deepest woe
had forgot thee [85-6].

The Greek man of action and heroic cunning has here been transformed into a blunt but likable next-door neighbor. The Greek hero whose sanity lay in the fact that he represented the law and order of the patriarchy has here become the rebel; his sanity exists in his ability to think and act, free from the corrupting ideology of the state.

As such he stands in stark dramatic opposition to the oppressive figure
of the establishment in the person of Aegisthus who appears on stage
"flanked by body guards." It is by virtue of his revolutionary activity
that this Orestes becomes a hero, for by means of his rebellion he in-
fuses new life into the old ideals (whatever they may represent for
Pound):

CHORUS

Aah!
Curses work out. They live who lie under ground,
The blood of the dead, long dead
Overwhelms their slayers.
And the dead hands
drip Mars, and the slain
blood, blood. I can't blame 'em [95].

The chorus reinforces this theme that seems to me to fall little short of
terrorism with its justification of "a few polite words," of cunning and
hypocrisy with which to mask the necessary deed of violence. Murder
and patricide have here lost all sense of mystery. Violence is a practical
matter, merely the job of the liberator:

ORESTES

You don't have to tell me how that bitch and Aegisthus
are running all dad's place to ruin
. . .
no time for all that
got to get on with the job.
Tell me the best way to get to it [86].

One cannot help wondering to what extent Pound is still influenced by his earlier Fascist convictions. In this play Orestes, though not
as invested with the violent emotional needs or experience of Electra,
is as willing as she is to do the deed; in fact, he is full of zeal for his
act of retribution:

ORESTES

It's a pity you can't all of you die like this
and as quickly, every one like you [102].

Far from experiencing any pangs of remorse, this hero, with the reserva-
tions that are characteristic of the present age, merely records an obligation well done:

ORESTES

All right, the house is clean again, if what Apollo
said is right [95].

Unlike his Sophoclean model, Pound's play ends with no unspoken questions hanging over the audience, no guilt, no horror, only
that sense of freedom that comes with a quiet conscience:

CHORUS

Delivered, Delivered
Swift end
So soon
Te Nun teleothen [103].

In her production, Carey Perloff boldly brings Pound's play into
the inner city of New York with much of the incumbent problems of
squalid, inner-city life. The set is a large, fenced area reminiscent at one
and the same time of the imprisoned physical and mental states of both
Pound and Electra and also of a basketball court which typically serves
as both recreation-center and jail for the urchins of downtown areas and
which, it has been noted, is suggestive of a sordid kind of "Greek Side
Story."[117] The costumes are evocative but timeless. Electra is dressed in
the shapeless black shift that we associate both with homelessness and
tragedy. Her shock of white hair contrasts with the blackness of her
dress and thereby, it has been suggested, accentuates the extreme
polarities of her essentially tragic outlook on life. She has been described as crow-like in her inwardness and her undeflectable sense of
purpose.[118] Clytemnestra appears on stage armed from top-to-toe in
the crude, pushy sexuality and false youthfulness of the upper-middle-
class Manhattan "homemaker." Thus, the enormous distance between
the mother and the daughter is brought home to the audience by
means of the disparity in their social and economic situations. Electra
expresses the full horror of her situation with chilling dignity:

ELECTRA

They say she's my mother [77].

At the same time there are definite insinuations in the text of child
molestation:

ORESTES

How? beats you? starves you?

ELECTRA

Yes, and everything else [77].

The chorus consists of a black woman and a white woman, two powerfully strong females who seem to vacillate between mother figures and prison matrons and who knit and do their paperwork as they guard over this inner-city scene.

In sharp contrast to them, the tutor speaks throughout in the heavy Irish brogue with which, once and for all, he demystifies Sophocles:

PYLADES

You BLOODY fools shut up
ain't you got ANY sense whatever
no more care for your lives? [88].

And Orestes is a black avenging hero and deliverer of the victims of city-squalor. It takes the combined efforts of all the disparate aspects of the city to save it from destitution and insanity.

Electra is the ruined child of her city desperately waiting for deliverance. Again, she is sharply contrasted to her sister: Chrysothemis lives on half-truths while Electra represents the uncompromising voice of an American ideal that has been swept under the rubble, under the savagery of the sprawling metropolis. Again, she is the tragic hero who willingly sacrifices her personal happiness in her single-minded pursuit of the moral ideal.

In a dramatic reversal of the black and white symbolism for good and evil that is customary in the Western tradition, this production seems to play upon the concept of vitality which is equally a cliché associated in Western literature with dark skin. Here, Electra's diminutive figure, her white hair and her rasping voice which is at times drained of all energy stand in sharp dramatic contrast to the strong, dark vitality, the new-blood, the fresh perspective of her brother. Electra's is the energy of true grit, of an indomitable spirit. She makes her first entrance by literally crawling onto the stage, and she clings to the sides of her cage with the will of the survivor. In this sense, again, Electra becomes Orestes: she, clinging desperately with the last vestiges of her strength and sanity to the solid values of an ideal that no one else can remember, and he, a new life-force, a new energy, the savior of his city.

Jack Richardson: *The Prodigal* (1960)

So far the Electra myth has been defined as the meeting of the old with the new. As such, the myth seems to recur at times of changing ideologies when it becomes necessary to rethink established precepts and institute new ones. Perhaps one of the reasons that there has been such a prevalence of Electra plays in our own century is that this has been a time of particularly rapid changes of ideology. It seems appropriate therefore to look for such a play in the 1960s, a period that epitomized the reevaluation of the old, and as such I mention *The Prodigal* by Jack Richardson.

In this rendition of the Electra theme, the prodigal son has been brought up under the myth of his father, a hero, a warrior and a tyrant and, like all the American sons of the sixties, the son wants to escape the destiny of the father.

But the father sails victoriously back into the harbor in an archetypal image of resurrection. He comes with "golden shields" that "reflected the sun into Electra's pained eyes."[119] He is the sun god, the sky god, image of the traditional, conquering, masculine hero. The issue here becomes one of separating the legend from the man, for, on this stage, the myth of his father becomes the reality of Orestes. He, and perhaps we of the audience, have related all these years not to the individual but to the abstraction, not to Agamemnon the man, but the myth. Any possibility of Orestes' having a personal relationship with his father has been shattered by the cruelty of the reputation that has preceded Agamemnon's homecoming: that the war hero had sacrificed his daughter and thousands of warrior's lives for the questionable "chastity" of Helen. Again masculine heroism implies aggression and the victimization of women. Given Agamemnon's reputation how can the son come to personal terms with the father?

ORESTES

Can laughter, can intimacy, can touch tell more about a man . . .
than the personal myth he bequeaths to us in death or absence? [213].

Orestes tells Electra:

ORESTES

We both have a legend and now we must undergo the often, painful
experience of seeing it turned into a man [226].

This is what *The Prodigal* does for us and did for the spectators of the 1960s. It turns the myth into reality, the hero into the antihero and the tragic form into a tale of a man trapped by the ethics of those that went before him.

In this play Clytemnestra, mythologically the cause of the Electra-Orestes tragedy, is fearful, uncomplicated and relatively unvindictive. Here she plays no part in a myth which is the product of an essentially masculine culture. Like Aegisthus in the play by Giraudoux, she is not made of the stuff of heroism but merely wants to inhabit the low ground. She justifies her disloyalty to her husband with the words:

CLYTEMNESTRA

I was never strong enough to stand beside you on mountain peaks and gaze with an impersonal eye at the world which you molded to suit your great ideas. . . . I belong on lower ground where seasons change and where small desires and thoughts are shared and understood. I belong to one who knows the love of this earth [231].

Agamemnon's virility and ambition frighten Clytemnestra because she recognizes in them their acquisitiveness and their destructive tendencies:

CLYTEMNESTRA

I pass by a pear tree. . . . I suddenly remember how he once climbed it to bring me the fruit from the highest branches. And the pool in front of the palace. . . . I recalled how Agamemnon used to enjoy throwing pebbles at its oversized fish. . . [223].

Aegisthus seems to recognize the distinction made in the first chapter of this work between himself as what we had termed the "personal father" and Agamemnon as the "transpersonal," for he acknowledges the essential difference between them:

AEGISTHUS

You love a man for what he might be; I for what he is. You glory in his potential. . . . I sympathize with his existence as it is now. . . . You cry for the heroic; I have tears of verse for the weak [236].

Do these two men represent the ideologically alienated generations of the 1950s and '60s? Do they represent the different political parties that comprise the American government? For his part, Orestes, as the product of a decade in which nothing is certain, admits to his father:

ORESTES

> It could be that I who believe nothing I would ask a dog to miss a
> meal for, envy you who are certain to the point of a thousand deaths
> [246].

Ultimately, myths are constructed upon authentic human attributes
and Agamemnon withstands the challenge of his son. His courage and
humanity prove to be richer than his reputation so that Orestes, against
his better judgment, is forced to recognize the humor and the nobility
of spirit of his father.

Agamemnon does not bring home a fiery-eyed visionary, an un-
tamed prophetess of doom as in the original form of the myth, but a
homely, middle-aged woman who works a wicker basket (as do the
archetypal female weavers of men's destiny from Homer to the present). This Cassandra sprouts sage little predictions. She is a comfortable
seer that instinctively guesses the outcome of events. The mythical
power of prophecy is thus reduced, in our own day, to female intuition.
Cassandra is a mother goddess who is comforting in her familiar aunt-
like guise. The diminished dramatic stature that she holds on this stage
provokes questions regarding the power that modern woman wields
over man's destiny and the position that she holds in today's Western
society. The archetypal image of visionary that this ironic figure suggests to us makes us question the power of the instincts and their place
within modern society. It makes us question why the opinions of
women go so unheeded in our rational, Western world.

As Martin Luther King, Jr., would have said, Agamemnon has
"slept through a revolution." He is a hero in a changed world. Yet, true
to his "heroic" character, Agamemnon predicts the tragic fates of
himself and his son, and recognizes within them the crucial turning
point of every son's life:

> My death will be a fact—there in front of you and you will step
> neither around nor over it [248].

For Agamemnon, self-realization means identification and responsibility. Masculine heroism is a struggle against nature and nature
does not guarantee its continuance. Agamemnon needs Orestes' promise of help, for his son is his only guarantee that his "heroic" vision will
be carried into the future.

But the son here is a young Hal who runs from responsibility and
seeks to hide his youth and innocence, and Pylades is a Falstaffian

character who encourages his friend's desire for freedom. Orestes is tempted to sail over the ocean (an image suggestive of death, the unconscious mind and, perhaps, baptism into a better life) with Praxithia and thereby escape from responsibility into fantasy. Cain-like, the prodigal son is exiled from mankind, ironically this time because he *refuses* to murder. This Orestes is prevented from pursuing his own vision of the simple unheroic life. Neumann writes:

> The absence of father identification prevents the eternal youth from ever obtaining his kingdom. His refusal to become a father and to assume power seems to him a guarantee of perpetual youth, for to assume power is to accept the fact that it must be passed on to a future son and ruler. The individualist is essentially nonarchetypal—that is to say, the eternal revolutionary, as he grows older, turns out to be a neurotic who is not prepared to "be his age" and accept his limitations. To negate the Isaac complex is not to get beyond it.[120]

From dramatic and mythical perspectives, the withdrawal of Orestes from society constitutes the precursor of the birth of the hero, an element of tragedy that we have recognized in all the previous forms of the myth. Ultimately Orestes' tragedy consists in his inability to free himself from the tethers of his masculine, hero-oriented culture:

ORESTES

The world demands that we inherit the pretensions of our fathers, that we go on killing in the name of ancient illusions about ourselves [261].

The pacifist is trapped in the vise of the classical world. The question is: Does he have the degree of tenacity required to loosen its hold?

Giraudoux had not allowed the tragic form to pull the audience under its emotional spell. Apart from the alienating characters of the beggar and the Furies, he had the gardener step completely out of the action and chat with the spectators. In Richardson's play, public opinion is no longer in the hands of the chorus, but in the hands of us—the audience. We are forced to become judges not only of the particular crime of Clytemnestra and Aegisthus but of tragedy and heroism as a whole. Talking directly to us Cassandra says:

CASSANDRA

Let us suppose the sea is our audience... [S]ome ... would have Orestes return ... to curse in public the back-stairs activities of his mother... [I]n the cheaper seats [they] think that progress must go

on.... [but] for the majority, dramatic justice . . . can be simply
solved by death. They speak with Electra's voice [262].

The unconscious, associated with the ocean waves that Cassandra
is addressing, is here no longer the Furies of Orestes, but is the conscience of the spectator. The moral dilemma of meaningless revenge
(tragedy) versus the simple life of man in nature has become our own
struggle and the tragedy of the prodigal son is that he is forced against
his will into a *Weltanschauung* that is no longer his own. Could
Richardson be referring also to the dilemma of the modern poet vis-à-
vis the classical form?

And what of Electra? Electra has remained throughout the intemperate voice of the past. She is the natural offspring of the heroic,
Western ideal that regards reality in stark terms of black and white. The
"golden shields" of her father are reflected in the pain of her eyes. Hers
is her father's ideal. For her there are the innocent and the criminals
and the criminals must be condemned. In this version of the myth, hers
is the intransigent world of the fathers.

Ideally there should be two parallel playing-areas here, one for the
stage-action and one for the spectators who, as the play progresses,
become as much a part of the action as the players. In fact, the spectators become players by virtue of their vital roles in assessing the archetypal questions of Orestes: questions of honor, family loyalty, personal
morality and integrity, public duty versus private vision, duty versus
impulsiveness, heroism versus antiheroism, murder versus guilt and the
tragic form versus the antitragic form. Does Orestes' flight from the
heroic constitute the betrayal of his father, his country, his honor? This
is not a "tragic" stage; it should be constructed in such a way as to reflect
the equal balance between the old heroic ideal and the new ideal of acceptance and pacifism. It should reflect the equality that exists between
the actors and the spectators and the dialectics that is encouraged between them during the performance.

Adrienne Kennedy:
Electra and *Orestes* (1980)

In her free translation of these two plays, Adrienne Kennedy
transforms Euripides' realistic use of language and his set that had em-
phasized the humble dignity of the Athenian peasant into a stark,

presentational repetition of the myth. The action is not introduced by the peasant in such a way as to reveal his character, but by the chorus as yet another record of ancient oral lore:

CHORUS

Our ancient city Argos. The river Inachus.

It was here that King Agamemnon led his army forth and with ships of war set sail for Troy.

And having killed the King of Troy and sacked that noble city he returned here to Argos. And on our temple walls hung high his trophies.[121]

It is the record of masculine conquest and violence. The style of this play seems to call for as bare a stage as possible. The language is impoverished, as is this latest version of the myth. It is the end result of a civilization of which it is characteristic. As such, this modern rendition reverts to the ritualistic; its language stylized and atonal.

In Kennedy's interpretation, Electra loses her neurotic features and becomes what is by now a stereotype of female determination and strength of character. Unlike her Euripidean counterpart, Electra here rejects the finery offered by the chorus of women, not out of self-pity but out of a genuine sense of mourning:

I cannot come. Fine dresses and necklaces of gold my dear friends, make my heart sadder. I could not bear the sight of the girls of Argos dancing, nor would I want to dance with them [E 108].

Yet after her liberation, she is ready to rejoice:

Set your feet dancing
Dance like the light.
. . .
My finery that I possess that is
stored in the cottage I will
bring out.
Too I will bring the crown
for my brother's head [E 131].

This, in a manner similar to that of Hofmannsthal's play, is a fiery and savage dance of victory. Yet the tone is somehow as dead as the soul that is capable of such an act of liberation. The beautiful robes that she has stored for this occasion are reminiscent of the deadly finery that Medea had used for her own revenge:

MEDEA

. . . They say the gods themselves
Are moved by gifts, and gold does more with men than words.
. . .
And give her the dress—for this is of great importance,
That she should take the gift into her hand from yours.[122]

The implication of Kennedy's translation is that heroism in our culture is synonymous with violence and that the gods are Western man's insurance that violence will be perpetrated:

ORESTES

Some monster disguised as a god has commanded me. But I can't believe what the god told me is right.

ELECTRA

You cannot lose your nerve and be the coward now. You must use the same deception she used when with Aegisthus' help she struck our father down.

ORESTES

I'll go in. Every step is dreadful and the deed before me still more dreadful yet if heaven so wills, let it be done [E 133–4].

Religion is an excuse for murder. Violence is perpetrated at every religious ceremony:

ELECTRA

Will you do this for me? Offer the tenth day sacrifice for a son.
. . .

CLYTEMNESTRA

Well as a favor, I'll go in and pay the gods the respect for your son. And then I must go to where my husband's sacrificing to the nymphs out in the pasture [E 136].

As a consequence of this, sorrow is also god-given:

CHORUS

Happiness is brief.
It will not stay.
God batters at its sails,
sorrow strikes,
and happiness goes down,
and glory sinks.[123]

European history is that of the Electra myth. Western culture perpetu-
ates itself by means of a religiously sanctioned violence:

CHORUS

> Glory decays, and
> greatest goes
> from the happy house of Atreus.
> Beneath the proud facade
> the long stain spread
> as the curse of blood began—
> strife for a golden ram,
> slaughter of little princes,
> a table laid with horror,
> a feast of murdered sons.
> And still corruption swelled,
> murder displacing murder,
> to reach at last
> the living heirs of Atreus [O 155–6].

Matricide is the natural culmination of such a history:

CHORUS

> What terror can compare with us?
> Hands of a son,
> Stained with his mother's blood [O 156].

In this version of the myth Orestes is not horrified by the savagery
of his sister, for here, despite his qualms when actually confronted with
matricide, the hero comes specifically to recruit his sister for the act of
murder:

ORESTES

> I must see her and get her help in executing our revenge [E 107].

In such a way, women are subsumed within the violent male ideology.
Here, the women of the Troy-Electra myths are victims of an all-encompassing, essentially alien, masculine culture, one that was founded
upon violence and that guarantees its future by means of the victimization and manipulation of its women:

ORESTES

> How could he be avenged?

PYLADES

Listen: we will avenge him by murdering Helen [O 159].

The irony of this latest version of the Electra myth is that it presents the hero as one who is brave enough to murder innocent women and children:

ORESTES

Seize her and stop her screaming. Let Menelaos learn what it is to fight with men, not cowards from Troy [O 166].

The gods are a projection of the male ego and have been created by men to legitimize their victimization of women:

APOLLO

Cease Menelaos. It is I Phoebus Apollo.
Helen is here with me. Orestes did not kill her.
Helen, being born of Zeus, could not die
and now will sit enthroned forever, a star for sailors.
It is Orestes' destiny to leave Argos and journey to
the city of Athena and give justice for his mother's
murder. The gods on the hill of Ares shall be his
judges and acquit him in a sacred verdict.
Then Orestes will marry Hermione.
Electra shall marry Pylades as promised.
Happiness awaits him.
Menelaos will be king in Sparta and I shall give Argos
to Orestes ... for it was I who commanded his mother's
murder. I compelled him to kill [O 171].

This ending belongs only to fairy tales. The men are guaranteed eternal happiness and the beautiful Helen is transformed from a woman into the abstraction of the masculine ambition.

On the subject of the male projection of the female onto objective reality, Simone de Beauvoir points out that:

Not only are cities and nations clothed in feminine attributes, but also abstract entities, such as institutions; the Church, the Synagogue, the Republic, Humanity are women....[124]

In fact, she is repeating the Freudian principle that such institutions, being receptacles, are symbols of female-sexuality. Simone de Beauvoir continues:

So ... are Peace, War, Liberty, the Revolution, Victory. Man feminizes the ideal he sets up before him as the essential Other, because woman is the material representation of alterity; that is why almost all allegories, in language as in pictorial representation, are women. Woman is Soul and Idea, but she also is a mediatrix between them; she is the divine Grace, leading the Christian toward God, she is Beatrice guiding Dante in the beyond, Laura summoning Petrarch to the lofty summits of poetry. . . . The gnostic sects made Wisdom a woman, Sophia, crediting her with the redemption of the world and even its creation. Here we see woman no longer as flesh, but as glorified substance; she is no longer to be possessed, but venerated in her intact splendor . . . through all the tradition of gallantry, woman is no longer an animal creature but is rather an ethereal being, a breath, a glow.

Beauvoir also says of man's regard for women: "If he is anxious to believe her pure and chaste, it is less because of amorous jealousy than because of his refusal to see her as a body." The male abstraction of the female, as we see in the myth of Helen, is, then, nothing more than the manifestation of his fear of her material nature.

Beauvoir quotes from medieval litanies to illustrate the idealization and desexualization of women within Christianity:

> . . . Most high Virgin, thou art the fertile Dew, the Fountain of Joy, the Channel of pity, the Well of living waters which cool our fervors.
> Thou art the Breast from which God gives orphans to suck. . . .
> Thou art the marrow, the tiny Bit, the Kernel of all good things,
> Thou art the guileless Woman whose love never changes. . . .
> Thou art the subtle Physician whose like is not to be found in Salerno or Montpellier. . . .
> Thou art the Lady with healing hands. . . . Thou makest the paralyzed to walk, thou reformest the base, thou revivest the dead.

With this, we have come full circle to the prehistoric, Egyptian representation of the all-encompassing and all-fecundating cow-goddess and goddess of the sky, yet ironically it is against this reduction of the real woman into an abstraction that Adrienne Kennedy, as modern woman, is struggling.

The other predicament of woman in a male society is that of Hermione, the trusting young girl who is so easily bartered by her father into the hands of her would-be assassin. The subject of this myth is, and probably has always been, the questioning of the ambiguous role that women hold in this otherwise perfectly ordered, consciously destructive society. Beauvoir says:

> Representation of the world, like the world itself, is the work of men;

they describe it from their own point of view, which they confuse with absolute truth.[125]

And what of the Amazon-like Clytemnestra and Electra? How, in the final analysis, do we come to terms with their violence? On the question of woman in this myth, in Greek theater and in theater in general Sue-Ellen Case writes:

> She definitely feels excluded from the conventions of the stage, bewildered by the convention of cross-gender casting, which is only practised for female characters. Mimesis is not possible for her. Perhaps the feminist reader will decide that the female roles should be played by men, as fantasies of "Woman" as "other" than man, as disruptions of a patriarchal society and illustrative of its fear and loathing of the female parts. In fact, the feminist reader might become persuaded that the Athenian roles of Medea, Clytemnestra, Cassandra and Phaedra are properly played as drag roles. The feminist reader might conclude that women need not relate to these roles or even attempt to identify with them. Moreover, the feminist historian might conclude that these roles contain no information about the experience of real women in the classical world. Nevertheless, the feminist scholar must recognize that theater originated in this kind of cultural climate and that the Athenian experience will continue to provide a certain paradigm of theatrical practice for the rest of Western theatrical and cultural history. By linking practice, text and cultural background in this new way, she may enhance her understanding of how the hegemonic structure of patriarchal practice was instituted in Athens.[126]

It is one thing to question whether women characters, as male creations, bear any similarity to their silent, off-stage counterparts, and whether women actors can actually play these characteristics as their own. Another, and, to my mind, much more acute requirement is to question the extent to which real women force themselves into these masculine models of femininity, as into a straightjacket, a straightjacket which is painful and which contorts the female shape even further from its true form. Perhaps it is time to turn our backs on the way in which the "hegemonic structure of patriarchal practice was instituted in Athens." Perhaps it is time to give up the myth, to liberate Electra. Perhaps it is time that women extricate themselves from the alien theatrical legacy that has been foisted upon them, from their male-given archetypes; that they separate the women from the Woman, that they look into their own mirror of femininity, learn their own movements, their own dance, their own story, their own theater. Perhaps when the truly female principle is released it will give birth to an entirely new and different Western civilization.

Electra has become a theater that challenges the moral right of the dominant culture to impose its myths upon its subjects. Far from the Aeschylean dependence on a shared worldview, writers of the 1980s and 1990s advocate diversity and decentralization as the democratic mode.

This is theater that exposes the lie inherent within the myth of the hero as an excuse for the perpetuation of masculine control. It is theater that exposes the god as a tool of the male power structure. In Kennedy's theater, maturation can take place only on the part of individual spectators as they become aware of their own intrinsic distance from the controlling mechanisms of the Establishment.

Heiner Muller: *Hamlet-Machine* (1984)

The final Electra play which I consider part of the deep-structure of the myth is the *Hamlet-Machine* by the eastern German playwright, Heiner Muller.

I am aware that there are many reinterpretations of *Hamlet* which have not been included in this study as Electra plays; however, I feel justified in including this play as such, because of the specifically schizophrenic treatment by which Muller deals with the characters of Hamlet and Ophelia, and because of the way in which he ultimately reduces the *Hamlet* theme into a dialectic between the masculine and feminine, in the persons of these two characters.

Muller's work is filled with violent, surrealistic and macabre images, expressions both of the turmoil, destruction and schizophrenia of his immediate German experience under Nazi rule, and the product of German history as a whole. It is theater torn between the conflicting emotions of a Marxist ideology to which he adheres and the experience of Communist brutality which became a reality in 1956 with Khrushchev's revelation of the worst excesses of Stalinism and with the invasion of Soviet forces into Hungary (violence that has been relived recently in China).

Muller is the quintessential German writer. His national and personal experiences have made him acutely conscious of himself as both victimizer and victim, as both Hamlet, the citizen that supports the brutality of oppressive regimes:

HAMLET

LET ME HELP YOU UP, UNCLE, OPEN YOUR LEGS, MAMA[127]

and Ophelia, eternal image of despair:

OPHELIA

I am Ophelia. The one the river didn't keep. The woman dangling from the rope. The woman with her arteries cut open. The woman with the overdose. SNOW ON HER LIPS. The woman with her head in the gas stove [54].

He is at the same time the poet (Orestes) — guilty because he is a passive witness to the horrors that have been perpetrated against his country (Electra) —

HAMLET

I'M GOOD HAMLET GI'ME A CAUSE FOR GRIEF
AH THE WHOLE GLOBE FOR A REAL SORROW
RICHARD THE THIRD I THE PRINCE-KILLING KING
OH MY PEOPLE WHAT HAVE I DONE UNTO THEE
I'M LUGGING MY OVERWEIGHT BRAIN LIKE A HUNCHBACK
CLOWN NUMBER TWO IN THE SPRING OF COMMUNISM
SOMETHING IS ROTTEN IN THIS AGE OF HOPE
LET'S DELVE IN EARTH AND BLOW HER AT THE MOON [53].

and Electra, the eternally female land that now, Gaia-like, rejects her children-lovers:

OPHELIA

Yesterday I stopped killing myself. I'm alone with my breasts my thighs my womb. I smash the tools of my captivity, the chair the table the bed. I destroy the battlefield that was my home. I fling open the doors so the wind gets in and the scream of the world. I smash the window. With my bleeding hands I tear the photos of the men I loved and who used me on the bed on the table on the chair on the ground. I set fire to my prison. I throw my clothes into the fire. I wrench the clock that was my heart out of my breast. I walk into the street clothed in my blood [54-5].

Ophelia-Electra is Armageddon. She is the new order that, in this instance, smashes the idols of the old. She is A-Lektra, the unmated, because in her bitterness she declares:

OPHELIA

I eject all the sperm I have received. I turn the milk of my breasts into
lethal poison. I take back the world I gave birth to. I choke between
my thighs the world I gave birth to. I bury it in my womb. Down with
the happiness of submission. Long live hate and contempt, rebellion
and death. When she walks through your bedrooms carrying butcher
knives you'll know the truth [58].

Ophelia, therefore, appears on stage as the inversion of the Virgin
Mother. In the form of the madonna with breast cancer, she rejects the
world of male-domination to which she has given birth. Horatio and
Hamlet "freeze under the umbrella, embracing. The breast cancer
radiates like the sun" (55).

In Oscar Wilde's *Salome*, the Electra-character had been identified
with the moon, symbol of beauty, madness, dangerous changeability,
and erotic female sensuality. But by the time we arrive at this play by
Muller, the violence of Western culture has transformed the entire
archetype of the female as we have always known her. Here, in self-
defense, in rage and in protest, the female breast—eternal image of
love and nurture—has become a source of poison, a fire equal to that
of the sun (image of the male and of masculine power) in its potential
for destruction.

Are the capitalized male speeches quoted above contrasted to the
small letters of Ophelia's speeches in a deliberate demonstration of
their relative roles in society, and should they be understood as such by
the actors?

I am tempted to digress, for a moment, from our Electra theme
in order to add yet another element to our expanding definition of
theater. To this end I quote from the words of the famous director of
political theater, Erwin Piscator, as he reminisces about his experiences
in the first world war:

Ypres—Belgium.
The shells whistle around our heads. The order is DIG IN! I am
lying on the ground, my heart beating madly, and like the others I
try to use my spade and dig into the earth.
The sergeant arrives, cursing, "Dig in, Piscator!"
"I can't."
Sergeant: "Why not?"
"I can't."
Sergeant (howling!): "What's your profession?"
"Actor."
I looked at the sergeant helplessly as I pronounced the word.

> What a fraud, what false ecstasy and elusive life of dreams! Sud-
> denly I felt less afraid of the falling shells around me than ashamed
> of being an actor.
>   Something was shattered forever: illusion. The curtain separating
> life from stage was torn away. Theatre, yes, but a different kind — not
> a stage, but a platform — theatre as an instrument to probe life and
> to come to grips with reality — not an audience, but a community.[128]

Muller also questions the validity and the purpose of the artist in
the face of battle. His theater brings dead philosophers on stage lectur-
ing behind tombstone-lecterns. As they philosophize, women — metaphors for the victims of a savage society — dangle on the stage from a
rope, expose themselves to the spectators with lacerated and bleeding
arteries while Hamlet the poet, together with the audience, look on as
visitors in a theater or a museum. Muller realizes that, as in life so in
theater, pain cannot be romanticized; it is personal and immediate:

> The author can't ignore himself anymore.... If I don't talk about
> myself I'll reach no one ... [16].

Hamlet is Muller. He is every citizen in a regime of violence and oppression. As such he rips Muller's portrait apart on stage:

HAMLET

> Somewhere bodies are torn apart so I can dwell in my shit. Some-
> where bodies are opened so I can be alone with my blood. My
> thoughts are lesions in my brain. My brain is a scar. I want to be a
> machine [57].

Machines of our domestic lives — a refrigerator and three television
sets — become repositories for our emotions. The refrigerator hums and
the televisions play silently on stage until the moment life ceases. Then
the refrigerator bleeds and the television sets go blank.
    Like Piscator, Muller dedicates his art to exposing to his audience
the horrors and the ambiguities of society. In contrast to Brecht, his
mentor, however, solutions to the political problems do not interest
him. Like Herbert Blau, he claims that art consists of raising the issues.
As such, all aspects of the Electra-Orestes question are granted equal
validity. Muller is equally horrified by the Hamlets as by the Falstaffs
of society and, though ashamed of the passive intellectual stance, he
would rather be a victim than an aggressor, an attitude which, ironically, is quintessentially intellectual:

OPHELIA

Do you want to eat my heart, Hamlet?

HAMLET

I want to be a woman [55].

According to Carl Weber in the Introduction to the play, Muller considers Hamlet's dilemma to be

> The German "split"; the "two souls dwelling in my breast" the archetypal German Dr. Faustus agonizes over; Hamlet, — "this 'very German' character," as Muller once said — torn apart by the contradictions of existence; the divided Germany of today's political map — no other German writer represents these schisms as boldly and clearly in his life and work [15].

Muller is the Hamlet that berates himself for his effete intellectualism in the face of a violent reality.

There are shades of Buchner's *Woyzeck* in this play, of a nightmarish reality in which Hamlet becomes the victim of his own mind. Indeed, Muller's theater might be viewed as the logical extension of Buchner's:

> Claudius — now Hamlet's father — laughs without uttering a sound, Ophelia blows Hamlet a kiss and steps with Claudius/HamletFather back into the coffin [55].

The ritual of this theater is, again, the gathering of disparate members of the community for a raising of issues common to all. Yet the post–Fascist mentality is wary of mass ideology. In this world, there are no answers. Hope for the survival of human values consists in honestly confronting the questions, not by means of a shared worldview, but by the unflinchingly independent assessment of the individual. As such, this is theater of alienation, a theater that labels its scenes (perhaps by means of placards) in order to keep the spectators on guard and separated from the performance. More than anything, perhaps, it is the theater of Jean Genet, theater of violent images which in this instance represent the victims of political horror as fellow perpetrators in an inescapable dance of death. It is a theater which depicts the divorce of the masculine from the feminine as the macabre fallout of that violence:

> An angel, his face at the back of his head: Horatio. He dances with Hamlet.

> The dance grows faster and wilder. Laughter from the coffin. On a
> swing, the Madonna with breast cancer [55].

In this theater we recognize the age-old Hippolytan misogyny, yet here
man's horror of the female has become an expression of his desire to
escape the guilt of his own violence:

HAMLET

> I would my mother had one less when you were still of flesh: I would
> have been spared myself. Women should be sewed up—a world
> without monsters. We could butcher each other in peace and quiet,
> and with some confidence, if life gets too long for us or our throats
> too tight for our screams [53].

We have defined the Orestean story as the journey of the individual toward manhood. In no version of the myth have we seen the
hero actually inherit his kingdom. All versions end with the horror that
is consequent to such an experience. When talking about Brecht,
Muller says:

> Out of revolutionary impatience with the immaturity of the condi-
> tions stems the trend to substitute the proletariat, a trend that leads
> to paternalism, the disease of all Communist parties. In defense
> against the anarchic-natural matriarchy, the re-construction of the
> rebellious son into the father-figure begins . . . [Weber's Introduc-
> tion, 18].

Muller is acutely aware of the regression that automatically occurs when
the son becomes the father, when the revolutionary becomes the
Establishment and when the poet achieves success and is raised to the
comfortable ranks of society. Consequently, this Hamlet-Orestes
refuses manhood. Paradoxically, to him the heroic stance manifests
itself in refusing to pick up the gauntlet. "I want to be a woman" is this
hero's way of maintaining his integrity in the face of experience.

VII

In all the plays that we have studied so far, the masculine and the feminine have been presented as dramatic metaphors for the contradictory impulses that rage within the human soul: impulses of creativity, passion and freedom versis the drive of "civilized" man toward control, reason and order. In all the above instances the playwrights have challenged accepted notions of justice, honor, patriotism, and the public versus the private conscience from within the deep-structure of the myth. In this chapter I will present two examples of what I consider to be *Electra* plays in which the playwrights deliberately deviate from the deep-structure of the myth, and I will question the possible reasons for their motivations.

T. S. Eliot: *The Family Reunion* (1939)

In this 1939 version of the Electra myth, Eliot provides his audience yet again with alternate realities, for he juxtaposes within the same text realism with ritual, and the poetic with the mundane. The directions state that "the scene is laid in a country house in the North of England" in a "drawing room, after tea . . ." and we are presented with the gentile family scene, the maidservant and the butler, which constitute the traditional paraphernalia of realistic theater. Yet within this structure there is a chorus of family members which, despite the realism of the situation, introduces on stage both a modern sense of metatheater and an almost classical sense of the unknown:

CHORUS

Why do we feel embarrassed, impatient, fretful, ill at ease,
Assembled like amateur actors who have not been assigned their
   parts?
Like amateur actors in a dream when the curtain rises, to find themselves dressed for a different play, or having rehearsed the wrong
   parts. . .[130]

These characters have been gathered for a simple dinner party, yet they sense a subtext for which they are not prepared. The uneasy sense of alienation that the members of this chorus feel toward their assigned roles mirrors, perhaps, the roles of the members of such a society, roles that are assigned at birth, but which don't always fit as they should.

There is an atmosphere of foreboding here, a suggestion of the uncanny and the unknown. The subtext of the chorus differs greatly from the surface text of social decorum, and we soon realize that the chorus, though ignorant of the fact, is in a liminal space not unlike the one in which Aeschylus' chorus had conjured up the spirit of the dead, or that in which Hamlet had confronted the spirit of his father:

CHARLES

I might have been in St. James's Street, in a comfortable chair rather
	nearer the fire.

IVY

I might have been visiting Cousin Lily...

GERALD

I might have been staying with...

VIOLET

I should have been helping...

CHORUS

Yet we are here at Amy's command, to play an unread part in some
	monstrous farce, ridiculous in some nightmare pantomime.

AMY

What's that? I thought I saw someone pass the window.
What time is it? [22].

The audience expects a play of domestic problems within a comfortable setting. In fact it is exposed to a re-examination of the structure of its society, and a suggestion that reality exists not within the familiar, but within an entire, untapped world of spiritual opportunity. As such, it is Charles—a spectre from another world, not the expected Arthur or John—who passes the window in this scene. He has been conjured up by this very chorus of unsuspecting household guests. The modern chorus differs from the classical one in that it is unaware that there is an alternate and perhaps more satisfying reality beyond their window.

As such, spirits are not here to comply to the wishes of the protagonists, but as some objective, arbitrary force, a force that is silent and unseen:

HARRY

How can you sit in this blaze of light for all the world to look at?
. . .
Do you like to be stared at by eyes through a window? [23].

Throughout the performance the characters, and no doubt the spectators, are driven to the wrong conclusions because they are unable to conceive the unfamiliar. As Agatha says:

AGATHA

Men tighten the knot of confusion
Into perfect misunderstanding,
. . .
Neglecting all the admonitions
From the world around the corner
The wind's talk in the dry holly-tree
The inclination of the moon
The attraction of the dark passage
The paw under the door [21].

Thus, within the alternate styles of poetry and prose, alternate modes of reality are suggested — and missed — by the limited vision of the characters within this play. It is unfortunate that Eliot's characters vacillate between the poetic and the prosaic to such an extent that they destroy the artistic integrity of the play and thereby disrupt the receptability of the audience. Mary, for instance, totters precariously from the sublime to the ridiculous:

MARY

. . . I should have known it;
It was all over, I believe, before it began;
But I deceived myself. It takes so many years
To learn that one is dead! So you must help me.
I will go. But I suppose it is much too late
Now, to try to get a fellowship? [117–8].

The immediate, almost petty practicality of the last one-and-a-half lines of this quotation jars as badly with the tone of the earlier lines, as an opera singer who sings off tune.

In this version of the myth Eliot cuts directly to the attraction-repulsion of the mother-son relationship. As such, the mother is not

portrayed in the traditional role as the murderess of her husband and
the mother who banishes the son from the maternal bosom. Rather,
here Amy is the deserted wife and the devoted mother who, Electra-
like, arrests all signs of the passage of time in her dedication to his
return. The return of the son constitutes the life of the mother:

AMY

I do not want the clock to stop in the dark.
If you want to know why I never leave Wishwood
That is the reason. I keep Wishwood alive
To keep the family alive, to keep them together,
To keep me alive, and I live to keep them [15–6].

By now the all-too-close ties, the almost suffocating proximity and
interdependence of relationships within the family constellation are
recognizable to us as characteristic of the *Electra* motif.

Amy's only crime is the willful, Clytemnestra-like tenacity which
Agatha recognizes in her:

AGÁTHA

. . . But you are just the same:
Just as voracious for what you cannot have
Because you repel it [113–4].

As we have noted, the mythical characters in this play are not
clearly defined, independent personalities; rather, they overshadow,
stint, and cling parasitically to each other, each usurping the space of
the other and, in so doing, suggesting that there is no possible room
for the individual. The chorus of Ivy, that plant which lives and climbs
on the success of others, and Violet, which blooms only in the shade
of others, is emblematic of the plight of the characters in their dependency and lack of differentiation. Harry's life bears the stamp of Agamemnon and Paris, of their inordinate fear of and dependency upon
the female. He had run from the misty, northern air of intellectual
blindness and stifled emotions (represented by Wishwood) and from
the overbearing will of his mother under the spell of a woman whom
he was soon compelled to murder—in fantasy, if not in reality.

It is Agatha who grants Harry a means of transcending the myopic
claustrophobia of domestic materialism, who gives him some insight
into that other realm, a realm that lies always beyond the socialized
grasp. It is she who shows him that reality is more expansive, more
multifaceted than it seems. Harry responds to Agatha with:

HARRY

I think I see what you mean,
Dimly—as you once explained the sobbing in the chimney
The evil in the dark closet, which they said was not there,
Which they explained away, but you explained them
Or at least, made me cease to be afraid of them [32].

Are we to understand the "sobbing in the chimney" and the "evil in the dark closet," from a Freudian perspective, as the pain of human intercourse and as Harry's fear of the female, a fear which is denied by society but regarding which Agatha had reassured him, thereby enabling him to leave Wishwood and marry?

The traditional plights of Agamemnon, Orestes and Paris merge into that of Harry in such a way as to emphasize that the domestic situation always constitutes a trap for the hero:

AGATHA

... I mean that at Wishwood he will find another Harry.
The man who returns will have to meet
The boy who left...

And it will not be a very jolly corner.
When the loop in time comes—and it does not come for
     everybody—
The hidden is revealed, and the specters show themselves [18].

The hero recognizes that

HARRY

... the last apparent refuge, the safe shelter,
That is where one meets them. That is the way of
     specters ... [110].

However far and long the hero runs, ultimately he is bound to return and to confront himself and his personal destiny within the mirror of his own nature. However long and arduous has been the Electrean struggle against the social structure and the mores of Western civilization, a moment of final reckoning with it does arrive, as it seems to do within this play, and with it comes the suggestion that perhaps, after all is said and done, the deep structure of this civilization does not adhere to the needs of every individual.

Agamemnon and Orestes are both destroyed when they return home. So is Harry, but Harry is not a hero for his community. Moreover, the seven-year absence from which Harry returns is more reminis-

cent of the undifferentiated experiences of Paris and Menelaos in the
Trojan War than of the preheroic state of Orestes. Amy says of Harry's
former wife:

AMY

She never wished to be one of the family,
She only wanted to keep him to herself
To satisfy her vanity. That's why she dragged him
All over Europe and half round the world
To expensive hotels and undesirable society
Which she could choose herself [20].

Again it is important to note that relationships in this play over-
lap, that the roles of mythical heroes, of heroism itself, is muddled and
unclear. Amy has the strength and the pathos of Clytemnestra, yet the
sense of loss that she has suffered for her husband and the devotion with
which she awaits the return of her son are characteristic of Electra.
Agatha is undoubtedly a Cassandra figure in her ability to see beyond
the materialism of everyday life, and in her opposition to Amy, yet she
is also Electra, for it is she who is responsible for having saved and exiled
Orestes. Observe the similarity between Agatha's blurring of the sen-
timents of love, closeness and death, with that which we had noted
earlier in Sophocles' Electra:

AGATHA

I did not want to kill you!
You to be killed! What were you then? only a thing called
    "life" —
Something that should have been mine, as I felt then.
. . .
. . . But I wanted you!
If that had happened, I knew I should have carried
Death in life, death through lifetime, death in my
    womb [100–1].

Mary is also Electra. She has been held against her will in this
house. She is a servant tied to the indomitable will of Amy. Yet Amy
holds Mary captive not in order to prevent her from marriage or to bar
her access to the Orestean figure, but for the specific purpose of
marrying her to him. The horror for this Orestes is not that he is divorced from his beloved sister-lover, but that he is destined to be confronted by her at every turn. Most strange of all, perhaps, is that it is
not the Clytemnestra figure that murders her husband, but—at least

symbolically—it is the reverse. It is not Electra's two sisters who epito-
mize the alternative fates of women in an aggressive, masculine world,
rather it is Arthur and John, the (reckless and the docile) younger
brothers of Harry. Here, it is the young boys who are unable to find
themselves in a world, forever dominated by their mother. Moreover,
Mary, the Electra figure, is not the tragic heroine that we have recognized so far as one that sacrifices life and love for the correction of a
moral imbalance in nature; she does not goad Harry into the murder
of his mother, but rather pleads with him to stay and protect himself
from the ravages of his own mind. She is Mary, a Christianized Electra,
gentle and asexual. Yet the fact that she is planted in this house as bait
for Harry makes us question her true nature. Is she harmless or simply
another tool of the domestic ideology and, as such, a cloaked-dagger?
Could this be, despite the poet's much publicized conservatism and his
initiation into the Anglican church, Eliot's subconscious suspicions of
the real function of Christianity within Western culture?

Whatever our interpretation, Eliot is surely taking a stand against
the typecasting of his characters and for the multifaceted nature, the
many possible roles, the diversity and complex potential within every
one of us.

The major similarity between the traditional versions of the myth
and this is, it seems, that Harry comes from a separate physical and
emotional space than that of the other characters. Throughout his life
he has been persecuted by Eumenides, by a fear and a torture (perhaps
of himself) that has driven him from traditional situations. A clarifica-
tion of Harry's dilemma and the turning-point of this action seems to
lie in his confrontation with Agatha:

AGATHA

There is a deeper
Organisation, which your question disturbs [97].
. . .

A curse is like a child, formed
To grow to maturity:
O my child, my curse . . .
You shall be fulfilled:
The knot shall be unknotted
And the crooked made straight [107].

I propose that this play is a deliberate inversion of the myth in its
original form for the purpose of untying the knot within which the
social structure of Western society binds its members.

In the beginning of this work I had noted that the original use of the term "virgin" referred to a woman who utilizes the physical sperm of a man but who, in fact, conceives by means of the inspiration of the spirit. Here we have the same situation but the genders are reversed. Harry's mother is but a physical vessel, a carrier for a son who is the spiritual child of Agatha:

HARRY

Tell me now, who were my parents?

AGATHA

Your father and your mother.

HARRY

You tell me nothing [98].

Agatha reveals her intimacy with Harry's father:

AGATHA

I remember
A summer of unusual heat
For this cold country [99].

and her feelings for his child:

AGATHA

I felt that you were in some way mine!
And that in any case I should have no other child [101].

Agatha, the spiritual mother, tells Harry that she has had to "fight for many years to win" her "dispossession." It is her revelation to him that sets him off on his own "heroic" journey toward "dispossession." In this sense, Harry bears a remarkable similarity to the hero of Robinson Jeffers' *Tower Beyond Tragedy*. True to the inverted tone of this version of the myth, here, for the first time, it is not the hero's separation from the maternal that prepares him for manhood within society, but, rather, it is his relinquishing of the maternal which prepares him for an alternate reality, a reality that necessitates the distancing of himself from society as he has known it:

HARRY

The things I thought were real are shadows, and the real
Are what I thought were private shadows. O that awful
    privacy
Of the insane mind! Now I can live in public.
Liberty is a different kind of pain from prison [103].

The turning-point of this work is Agatha's revelation to Harry that his father had wanted to murder his mother. In this revelation Harry recognizes the feelings that he had harbored toward his own former wife and, perhaps, to women in general:

HARRY

. . . Family affection
Was a kind of formal obligation, a duty
Only noticed by its negelct. One had that part to play.
After such training, I could endure, these ten years,
Playing a part that had been imposed upon me;
And I returned to find another one made ready—
The book laid out, lines underscored, and the costume
Ready to be put on [103].

Perhaps it is his sudden realization that the woman's role in domestic society is as vulnerable and as circumscribed as the male's that frees Harry from his sense of obligation:

HARRY

When other people seemed so strong, their apparent
    strength
Stifled my decision. Now I see
I might even become fonder of my mother—
More compassionate at least—by understanding.
but she would not like that [103].

The world of this play is not the patriarchal one that we have observed so far, but a domestic world that is dominated by the female and that allows for no spiritual space. As such, sexual roles are reversed. This Agamemnon murders this Clytemnestra in an act of ultimate frustration. The hero's siblings are boys whose growth has been stunted by an overly dominant mother, and the hero himself is forced into flight by the claustrophobic hold that the female has over him. In this play, it is the rape of the male by the female that causes the hero to seek an alternative. Amy admits to Agatha, her spiritual counterpart, so attractive to her husband and her son:

AMY

You knew that you took everything
Except the walls, the furniture, the acres;
Leaving nothing — but what I could breed for myself
. . .
. . . What of the humiliation,
Of the chilly pretences in the silent bedroom,
Forcing sons upon an unwilling father?
. . .
I *would* have sons, if I could not have a husband:
Then I let him go. I abased myself [113; emphasis added].

With this we have come almost full circle to the modern, unromanti-
cized version of the queen bee, a mother-goddess who is disem-
powered, who simply relinquishes her mate after a forced and loveless
coitus. Ironically, with this conversion of the myth from a patriarchal
to a matriarchal society, we arrive, again, at man's most primordial
dilemma: can the male wrench immortality from the female by means
of his intellectual or spiritual activity? Is he able to move beyond the
traditional and the socially-prescribed, beyond the female and the
domestic — and relinquish himself to a new way of life?

Sam Shepard:
Curse of the Starving Class (1978)

We have defined the deep-structure of the Electra myth as one in
which the Orestean figure is forced to take a stand against the establishment, as one in which the focal point of action is always the meeting
of the old (Agamemnon) with the new (Orestes), as one in which the
play is propelled into action by the meeting of the male (Orestes) with
the female (Electra), as one in which Electra represents filial loyalty, in
which the Clytemnestra figure is "tainted" and always a mother manqué, as one in which the figure of Aegisthus is characterized by a lack
of idealism or any sense of the spiritual and as one in which the
Orestean figure approaches the action from a separate physical or psychological space than that of the other characters.

We have said that in this myth the figure of Aegisthus has usurped
the position of the Agamemnon both in the political arena and in the
affections of the Queen, that the figure of Clytemnestra is one whose
affections are diverted from her children and directed toward the one

who is presently in power, that the Electra figure is, by definition, the unmated, the imprisoned and the vengeful, and that the Orestean youth is the son and heir of Agamemnon and the would-be avenger of his father's murder.

In *Curse of the Starving Class* the royalty of the classical world has been reduced to a Californian family, characterized more by its painful obscurity and lack of gainful employment than by any positive social quality. Its members belong to a recognizable tribe of American nomads that migrate to the West in the hope of instant, free fame and fortune. From this perspective Weston's alcoholic bouts away from home and his futile attempts to buy cheap land in Palm Springs represent the last American vestiges of classical heroism:

WESTON

I just went off for a little while. Now and then. I couldn't stand it here. I couldn't stand the idea that everything would stay the same. That every morning it would be the same. I kept looking for it out there somewhere. I kept trying to piece it together. The jumps. I couldn't figure out the jumps. From being born, to growing up, to droppin' bombs, to having kids, to hittin' bars, to this. It all turned on me somehow. It all turned around on me. I kept looking for it out there somewhere. And all the time it was right inside this house.[132]

In contrast to the above, the ability of the Greek heroes to leave their families for ten years of heroic warfare seems so easy. Within the context of Greek heroism there was not as great a need to "figure out the jumps." For them, "droppin' bombs" was their way of ensuring a manhood worn thin within the narrow confines of domesticity. It was their way of maintaining control, of ensuring that life did not "turn on them." Despite their differences, neither hero—the modern or the Greek—is able to withstand the deadliness that awaits him within the home.

But what of the home? Ella is a far cry from the Greek Clytemnestra. Though a mother manqué, she does not consort with Taylor as a means of maintaining control over an abandoned kingdom, but rather as a possible means of escape from all responsibilities. The lights first go up on a battered house. There is no front door and within the first few sentences we learn that the door has been burst from its hinges in a confrontation between the drunken man of the house who was trying to enter and his wife who had bolted it against him. Like Clytemnestra, Ella has resented her husband's desertion and now resents the fact that he has returned to resume his authority over her.

This home that has been destroyed from within is now vulnerable, both literally and symbolically, to any passing predator.

The broken house has land, an orchard, even some livestock, yet all the images associated with them are images of devastation and neglect. The avocadoes are rotten, the livestock diseased, the tractor in disrepair, the land is neglected and the sheep castrated and diseased.

The family congregates in the kitchen. Ella is the epitome of female alienation and maternal neglect. It is the kitchen, "the warmest part of the house," that represents the hearth as the female nurturing center of the home, and the central shrine of this home is the refrigerator, symbol of the excruciating, indefinable pangs of hunger from which this family suffers. It is this sterile and mostly empty machine that constitutes the mother-substitute in a family that is alienated from any understanding of community, that has no roots, no center and no sense of self. The major activity throughout the play is the constant opening and shutting of the refrigerator door:

WESTON

Slams all day long and through the night. SLAM! SLAM! SLAM! What's everybody hoping for, a miracle! IS EVERYBODY HOPING FOR A MIRACLE? [157].

The poverty of this family is not that of the dignified peasant that we had seen in Euripides' *Electra*, but a source of shame. Emma begs the refrigerator:

EMMA

Any corn muffins in there? Hello! Any produce? Any rutabagas? Any root vegetables? Nothing! It's all right. You don't have to be ashamed. I've had worse. I've had to take my lunch to school wrapped up in a Weber's bread wrapper. That's the worst. Worse than no lunch [150].

The dishonor lies in the family's insensitivity to the promise of life that lies within their grasp. Their home, their land and their family abound with images of potential fruitfulness from the lambs that they castrate to Emma, the daughter with "the curse," the ability to give birth "the first time around" (155). They neglect the fertile land on which they live, preferring to set their dreams on arid desert sand in the vague hope of instant, unearned wealth. Weston's family hungers for the most basic commodities: for food, for identity, for a sense of belonging, a feeling of worth and purpose, yet he brings home artichokes from the desert. Like Agamemnon, he spurns the immediate for the intangible, the material for the dream. Ultimately, this family falls victim to the Taylors, the Ellises, the Emersons and the Slaters because they want to, because they buy into the sterile materialism of nameless, rootless strangers:

TAYLOR

Of course it's a shame to see agriculture being slowly pushed into the background in deference to low-cost housing, but that's simply a product of the times we live in. There's simply more people on the planet these days. That's all there is to it. Simple mathematics. More people demand more shelter. More shelter demands more land. It's an equation. We have to provide for the people some way [153].

The absurdity, of course, is that they are not providing for the people.

Ella is a mother manqué in the fullest sense of the word because, like Euripides' Phaedra, she has assumed as her own a dominant ideology that runs counter to her own nature:

ELLA

Now I know the first thing you'll think is that you've hurt yourself. That's only natural. You'll think that something drastic has gone wrong with your insides and that's why you're bleeding. That's only a reaction. But I want you to know the truth. I want you to know all the facts before you go off and pick up a lot of lies. Now, the first thing is that you should never go swimming when that happens. It can cause you to bleed to death. The water draws it out of you.
    . . . The next thing is sanitary napkins. You don't want to buy them out of any old machine in any old gas station bathroom. I know they say "sanitized." They're filthy in fact. . . . You don't know whose quarters go into those machines. . . . They're not hospital clean that's for sure. And you should know that anything you stick up in there should be absolutely hospital clean [138–9].

The "zombies" that dupe Weston and Ella out of their home are agents of the dominant ideology. It is an ideology that rejects the life-cycle, represented by the land, the orchard, the sheep, and by Emma's menarche in preference to the plastic sterility of urban life.

Emma's own fear of sexuality bears an uncomfortable similarity to that of Euripides' Hippolytus:

EMMA

Suddenly everything changed. I wasn't the same person anymore. I was just a hunk of meat tied to a big animal. Being pulled [148].

In the thousands of years that have elapsed since the Greek play, human dependence on its own nature has not changed. Neither has the human struggle against it. The only means Emma has of transcending her mother's hold over her and of escaping the trap of this unsavory family environment lies in her direct confrontation with her greatest fear and in her manipulation of it toward her own ends:

EMMA

I got out.

WESLEY

I know, but how?

EMMA

I made sexual overtures to the sergeant. That's how. Easy [196].

As we have seen in all the forms of this myth, it is the divorce of A-lektra, the unmated, from the natural cycle of life and the repression of her own sexuality that forces her into violence. Ironically, that violence is achieved here, by means of an explosion of sexuality that is commensurate only with the degree of the repression from which she has suffered.

EMMA

I'm going into crime. It's the only thing that pays these days....

It's the perfect self-employment. Crime. No credentials. No diplomas. No overhead. No upkeep. Just straight profit. Right off the top [196-7].

Profit, after all, is the main goal of all the characters in this play.

Freedom from the demands of nature is the ultimate goal of all the characters, even of Wesley who, at least for the present, fights for the preservation of the home. Even in this play there is a suggestion of the brother-sister-lover relationship, a proposal on the part of Emma that if the feuding parents would disappear, she and her brother could live harmoniously together. Wesley, however, wants to remove himself as far as possible from the complications of nature and of the human bond:

EMMA

... Maybe they'll never come back, and we'll have the whole place to ourselves. We could do a lot with this place.

WESLEY

I'm not staying here forever.

EMMA

Where are you going?

WESLEY

I don't know. Alaska, maybe. . . .

EMMA

What's in Alaska?

WESLEY

The frontier.

EMMA

Are you crazy? It's all frozen and full of rapers.

WESLEY

It's full of possibilities. It's undiscovered.

EMMA

Who wants to discover a bunch of ice? [163].

Like Harry in *The Family Reunion*, it is on his final return that the hero is forced to confront what in Jungian terms might be called his "Shadow," his true self, and his ultimate needs, only here it is the father, not the son, that attempts to find himself and the Eumenides of his conscience do not thrust him from his home, but reveal to him the promise of self-cultivation. Unfortunately, in this case, it is a promise that he is unable to bring to fruition.

For both Weston and Ella, the table at center-stage represents the altar of the dead hero that we had witnessed in ancient theater. For both characters are emotionally and spiritually dead, dead to their needs as human beings and to their human obligations. Around them in their figurative deaths congregate the predators. Weston and Ella have both relinquished charge over their own lives and, in these separate moments of symbolic death, others cluster over their bodies, chaos and violence take over, submerging the space that they had held in life in a macabre dramatization of the relentlessness of time and of the anonymity of an existence that has staked no claim on the living. In the absence of the father the alienated mother takes a stand. It is Wesley, the son, that comes to the defense of Weston:

WESLEY

I wouldn't wake him up if I were you.

ELLA

He can't hurt me now! I've got protection! If he lays a hand on me, I'll have him cut to ribbons! He's finished!

WESLEY

He's beat you to the punch and he doesn't even know it.

ELLA

Don't talk stupid! And get this junk out of here! I'm tired of looking at broken doors every time I come in here.

WESLEY

That's a new door.

ELLA

GET IT OUT OF HERE!

WESLEY

I told you, you better not wake him up.

ELLA

I'm not tiptoeing around anymore. I'm finished with feeling like a foreigner in my own house. I'm not afraid of him anymore [173].

Wesley, the Orestean figure of this play, is the one character who fights throughout to protect the family home. As the play opens we see him picking up the shards of the broken door, remnants of the battle of the sexes that had raged between his parents. As the play ends, Wesley remains on stage, protecting Ella from knowledge of her daughter's death. He stands in stark opposition to the narrow material-ism of Taylor (Aegisthus), loyal rather to that love of the living that Weston really represents but which has been buried beneath the temp-tation of a "quick and easy buck."

WESTON

What's the matter with the lamb?

WESLEY

Maggots.

WESLEY

Poor little bugger. Put some a' that blue shit on it. That'll fix him up [159].

For Wesley, although he might dream ultimately of reaching the icy regions of Alaska, there has been no radical denial of nature. On the contrary, it is he that has tried to restore the maggot-infested lamb to life. But he has been as determined by biological and social factors as the other members of his family, for ultimately the "nitroglycerine" that courses through his father's veins ignites him, too, into madness. The curse, the madness that is upon him is that he is destined to become his father, and it is his recognition of this that causes him to salvage, as his own, his father's discarded clothes and to murder the sacrificial lamb that he had brought on stage as symbol of both men:

WESLEY

And every time I put one thing on it seemed like a part of him was growing on me. I could feel him taking over me. . . .
    I could feel myself retreating. I could feel him coming in and me going out. Just like the change of the guards.

EMMA

Well, don't eat your heart out about it. You did the best you could.

WESLEY

I didn't do a thing.

EMMA

That's what I mean.

WESLEY

I just grew up here [196; emphasis added].

The pathos of Wesley's situation lies in this play's deviation from the deep-structure of the Electra myth. Ultimately Wesley does not come from another space. It is possible that his parents were just like him when they started out in life. As their son, his future is as determined as was theirs. He grows into their curse, their spiritual poverty and their foul smell as he puts on the old, soiled clothes his father has discarded.

The pathos of Wesley's life lies in the fact that he is not a hero, that he does not challenge the values of his parents and that he does not entertain any vision of his own. For him there has been no rupture with the female, no rebellion against the maternal. Only acceptance.

The play closes with Wesley and his mother together on stage, sole survivors of their family. If this had been any other version of the Electra myth it might be claimed that the mother-son togetherness depicted here represents the ultimate desire of the son to be bonded with his mother. But in this play of myopic vision, it merely represents the last remnants of the falling apart of the family structure. This Orestean figure, on stage with his mother, does not realize the much sought after heroic struggle or the heroic ideal, for Wesley, like his father, is no more than the sum and the victim of social factors.

The sleep of the parents might also represent their separate dreams. It might, in fact, be directed on stage as their stepping back and finally taking account of their lives as their way of recognizing within their respective responsibilities the potential for that meaning and that sense of belonging for which they have so much hungered. Thus, on awakening, Weston starts anew and Ella assumes, albeit momentarily, her responsibility to her daughter. Yet it is at this moment of awakening that both are cruelly confronted by "fate," by the hereditary curse of their family and of the human, social condition. It is the curse that Ella had recognized when first confronted with the fact that Weston had beat her to the sale of their house:

ELLA

Do you know what this is? It's a curse. I can feel it. It's invisible but it's there. It's always there. It comes onto us like nighttime. Every day I can feel it. Every day I can see it coming. And it always comes. Repeats itself. It comes even when you do everything to stop it from coming. Even when you try to change it. And it goes back. Deep. It goes back and back to tiny little cells and genes. To atoms. To tiny little swimming things making up their minds without us. Plotting in the womb. Before that even. In the air. We're surrounded with it. It's bigger than government even. It goes forward too. We spread it. We pass it on. We inherit it and pass it down, and then pass it down again. It goes on and on like that without us [173–4].

It is the curse of the house of Atreus. It is the curse of accumulated deeds that do not recognize a change of heart but which come relentlessly to exact retribution:

WESTON

YOU UNDERSTAND ME? IT'S ALL OVER WITH BECAUSE I'VE BEEN REBORN. I'M A WHOLE NEW PERSON NOW! I'm a whole new person.

WESLEY

They're going to kill you.

WESTON

Who's going to kill me! What're you talking about! Nobody's going to kill me!

WESLEY

I couldn't get the money.

WESTON

What money?

WESLEY

Ellis.

WESTON

So what?

WESLEY

You owe it to them.

WESTON

Owe it to who? I don't remember anything. All that's over with now.

WESLEY

No, it's not. It's still there. Maybe you've changed, but you still owe them. . . .

WESTON

I can't run out on everything.

WESLEY

Why not?

WESTON

'CAUSE THIS IS WHERE I SETTLED DOWN! THIS IS WHERE THE LINE
ENDED. RIGHT HERE. I MIGRATED TO THIS SPOT! I GOT NOWHERE
TO GO TO. THIS IS IT!

WESLEY

Take the Packard [192–3].

It is the curse of a world of predators in which all are interlocked, not
in a sense of community for the common good, but in a deathly struggle for personal, separate survival:

WESLEY

And that eagle comes down and picks up the cat in his talons and carries him screaming off into the sky.

ELLA

. . . And they fight. They fight like crazy in the middle of the sky.
That cat's tearing his chest out, and the eagle's trying to drop him,
but the cat won't let go because he knows if he falls he'll die.

WESLEY

And the eagle's being torn apart in midair. The eagle's trying to free
himself from the cat, and the cat won't let go.

ELLA

And they come crashing down to the earth. Both of them come
crashing down. Like one whole thing [200].

The characters within *Curse of the Starving Class* make desperate
attempts to free themselves from the mundane, but are ultimately
dragged back into the bog of their everyday struggle. As a reflection of
this, the style makes repeated attempts at poetry but is inextricably
governed by the depressing prose, by the realism that is characteristic
of an unheroic age. It is a style that reflects the particular deviation from

the deep structure of the Electra myth that characterizes *Curse of the Starving Class*. For the deviation consists precisely in the protagonist's inability to reach new vistas, in the fact that Wesley has never and can never reach a separate physical or psychological space from those of the people who share this home—the home that he loves so much.

The play is hilariously funny in parts. It is the humor of comedy and as such it alienates the spectators from the pain of the action to the extent that they can recognize it and laugh at it as their own.

Conclusion

The ritual of theater constitutes a raising of issues, a giving of physical form to the intangible realities of our lives which we would otherwise ignore. Theater thus "makes the invisible visible" in such a way as to enable us to examine our values, our nature and our judgment. It is the constant return of spectators to the sacred center of performance, and each performance necessitates, like the final return of Harry in *The Family Reunion*, the confrontation of ourselves with our Eumenides, our conscience or our "Shadow." As in Jack Richardson's *The Prodigal*, we, the audience, constitute as integral a part of the action as the actors, for the conflict of theater, once it is given form, becomes our own struggle. Do we reject the values that have been handed down to us and attempt to establish new ones, as did the Prodigal in Richardson's play, or as did Harry in the play by Eliot, or do we passively accept the dictates of the past with the subjection and the victimization that this entails (*Curse of the Starving Class*)? Are we as indifferent to the issues as the hero of Giraudoux' play, or do we take up the gauntlet of human concerns, as did Sartre's Orestes and suffer thereafter from the pain of human history and social concern?

What of the issue of ritual in the twentieth century? We have made mention of the concern of modern dramatists to counteract the passivity of an estranged, bourgeois audience. It has taken the contradictory geniuses of Artaud and Brecht to provoke modern spectators and to stimulate live, meaningful theater in our time. But neither's theory stands alone. Artaud's theater stimulated the emotions and the passions but, as Professor Mclain says in his article when speaking about the powerfully stimulating succession of images in television's rock video, "Does this vivid succession of images really substitute for the meaningful grappling with a story?"[137] Does the pricking of one's emotions, one's passions, even one's sensuality constitute the total theatrical event? On the other hand, is it not generally recognized that, despite the unchallenged validity of Brecht's intellectual theater of alienation, Brecht's own theater only really works when one is (as one undoubtedly is) pulled emotionally into the soul-striving, the human dilemmas of his characters? For the modern audience that is no longer tied to the action in the same manner as the ancient Greeks, by means of a shared religious belief, successful theater makes visible on stage an energy which is at once both intellectual and emotional. It is this that draws the audience repeatedly from the cinema houses and the television screens, it is this return and bonding of the audience with the actors which constitutes the ritual of live theater for the modern age.

Pirandello forced the issue of human nature on to his stage by lifting the mask of language (that rationalizing, regulating, covering mechanism) from our actions, by revealing beneath this superimposed order the essential chaos of our human condition. Yet we must acknowledge that men and women have attempted to stratify their chaos since their first attempts to utter sound, and that therefore, language—the human longing for order—is by now as legitimate an aspect of our natures, as is the chaos within our minds. The Nietzschean conflict between the Apollonian and the Dionysian, the rational and the instinctual, has raged for as long as we can trace the human line. Theater is the presentation of that conflict. It is the play of life itself. Chaos and order, images and words, emotions, ideas and themes, the sensual, the sexual and the spiritual—all claim equal hold on the theatrical platform. The actor, as the messenger of his or her community, seeks out all the polarities and complexities of the human condition. It is these things that the emerging hero confronts, and it is with these that the spectators have to grapple. Michael Mclain claims that theater is the ritual sacrifice of the actor for the creation of something meaningful in the minds of the spectator-community.[138] The actors create violence and conflict on stage in order, shaman-like, to give body to the spiritual subtext of our existence. As such, theater is still the sacred round of the original Greek ampitheater and, as such, the spectators of today's theater constitute as much a community as did those of ancient Greece.

Tout ça change, tout c'est la même chose. Throughout the many variations of the myth that we have studied in this work—even that of *The Family Reunion*, in which Electra was not rebellious against the mother-figure, or that of *Curse of the Starving Class*, which deviates from the deep-structure of the myth in that there is no significant break from the maternal on the part of Wesley the Orestean figure—the issues have remained consistent. It is, throughout, the artificial divorce of the male from the female that represents the human being's alienation from nature, and it is this alienation that constitutes the cause of violence and destruction in our culture.

The primal deed of heroism — the slaying of the maternal dragon by the adolescent and his attempts to combat the restraints of the repressive, all-too present Aegisthean father-figure while claiming as his own the vision of the heroic spirit — becomes the legacy of the male adolescent as he emerges into manhood. If we are to read these plays correctly it is a masculine struggle, fated to recur in each successive generation for it is a struggle that provides the only measure of control (even if only an illusory one) that the male has over his environment. It is a struggle that is imbedded only within an all-masculine nature, one that necessitates and suffers as a result of the artificial divorce of the feminine from the masculine within the individual. It is a struggle which constitutes — and constantly shatters — the bedrock of our civilization, and one which has twisted our history into a record of masculine violence.

What about the voiceless nature of women throughout this history? If our culture would have recorded equally the emotional needs, the social development, the struggle and the dreams of women and of men, and not regarded men as the personification of all peoplekind, if the male had allowed the feminine a place both within his personal, psychological structure — and within his political outlook, or, to press the point, if men had not wrenched themselves so ruthlessly from the female, would Western history not have been a totally different story?

The question from our present day perspective is: does our own hard-driving, masculine, and still sexist Western society derive its nature from the unconscious fears experienced by the Classical Greek male in earliest childhood? If so, will we ever be able to rid ourselves of its violence?

Notes

Introduction

1. Joseph Campbell, *Primitive Mythology: The Masks of God* (New York: Penguin Books, 1987), p. 4.
2. Claude Levi-Strauss, "The Structural Study of Myth," in *Structural Anthropology* (New York: Basic Books, 1963), pp. 207–31.
3. Levi-Strauss, p. 217.
4. Theodor H. Gaster, "Myth and Story," in *Sacred Narrative* (Berkeley: University of California Press, 1984), pp. 110–36.
5. Gaster, p. 112.
6. T. S. Eliot, "The Perfect Critic," in *The Sacred Wood* (New York: Methuen, 1920).
7. Gaster, pp. 125 and 128.
8. Levi-Strauss, pp. 206–31.
9. Mircea Eliade, *The Myth of the Eternal Return, or, Cosmos and History*, trans. Willard R. Trask (Princeton, N.J.: Princeton University Press, 1974).
10. Geza Roheim, *The Gates of the Dream* (New York: International Universities Press, 1952), p. 401.
11. Levi-Strauss, pp. 207–31.
12. Peter Brook, *The Empty Space* (New York: Atheneum Press, 1984), p. 42.

I

13. Erich L. Neumann, *The Great Mother* (Princeton, N.J.: Princeton University Press, 1974), p. 18.
14. Carol Gilligan, *In a Different Voice* (Cambridge, Mass.: Harvard University Press, 1982), p. 6.
15. Erich L. Neumann, *The Origins and History of Consciousness* (Princeton, N.J.: Princeton University Press, 1973), p. 131.
16. Andersen, *Myths and Legends of the Polynesians*, pp. 367–8, quoted in Neumann, p. 103.
17. Isaiah Tishby, "The Doctrine of Evil and the 'Klipah' in the Lurian Cabala," quoted in Neumann, *The Origins and History of Consciousness*, pp. 119–20.
18. Barbara G. Walker, *The Woman's Encyclopedia of Myths and Secrets* (San Francisco: Harper & Row, 1983), p. 1049.
19. Neumann, p. 132.
20. Aeschylus, *The Oresteia* (New York: Penguin Books, 1977), p. 161. Hereafter, quotations from this edition will be indicated by page number references in parentheses or brackets.

21. Jan Kott, *The Eating of the Gods* (Evanston, Ill.: Northwestern University Press, 1987), p. 254.

22. William Ridgeway, *The Origin of Tragedy* (New York: Benjamin Blom, 1966).

23. Eliade, p. 34.

24. Homer, *The Odyssey: The Story of Odysseus*, trans. W. H. D. Rouse (New York: New American Library, 1937), p. 36.

25. Levi-Strauss, p. 217.

26. Eliade, p. 35.

27. Eliade, p. 35.

28. Herbert Blau, *Take Up the Bodies: Theater at the Vanishing Point* (Chicago: University of Illinois Press, 1982), p. 83.

29. Northrop Frye, *Anatomy of Criticism: Four Essays* (Princeton, N.J.: Princeton University Press, 1973), p. 217.

30. Homer, *The Odyssey: The Story of Odysseus*, trans. W. H. D. Rousee (New York: New American Library, 1937), p. 39.

31. Aristotle, *Poetics*, trans. Gerald Elese (Ann Arbor: University of Michigan Press, 1970), p. 27.

32. Michael Grant, *The Rise of the Greeks* (New York: Macmillan, 1987), p. 30.

33. Grant, pp. 30–1.

34. Euripides, *Orestes and Other Plays* (Middlesex, England: Penguin Books, 1983), p. 333.

35. Grant, p. 31.

36. Euripides, *Hippolytus* in *Ten Plays*, trans. John McLean (New York: Bantam Books, 1985), pp. 80–1. Hereafter cited as *Hippolytus*.

37. *Hippolytus*, pp. 78–9.

38. Grant, p. 31.

39. Philip E. Slater, *The Glory of Hera* (Boston: Beacon Press, 1968).

40. Slater, p. 25.

41. Slater, p. 103.

42. Slater, pp. 16 and 13.

43. Slater, pp. 186–7 and 187.

44. Slater, pp. 13 and 25.

45. Slater, p. 31.

46. Slater, pp. 91 and 89.

47. Edward Tripp, *The Meridian Handbook of Classical Mythology* (New York: New American Library, 1970), p. 248.

48. Arnold Van Gennep, *The Rites of Passage* (Chicago: University of Chicago Press, 1960), pp. 92–3.

II

49. Sophocles, *Electra*, in *Electra and Other Plays*, trans. E. F. Watling (New York: Penguin Books, 1978), pp. 87–8. Hereafter, quotations from this edition will be indicated by "Watling," and a page number reference, in parentheses or brackets.

50. Thomas Woodard, "The Electra of Sophocles," in *Orestes and Electra*, ed. William M. Force (Boston: Houghton Mifflin, 1968), p. 281. Hereafter, quotations from this edition will be indicated by "Force," and a page number reference, in parentheses or brackets.

51. H. D. F. Kitto, *The Greeks* (New York: Penguin Books, 1986), p. 89.

52. Kott, p. 267.

53. Blau, p. 4.

III

54. Euripides, *Electra*, in David Greene and Richmond Lattimore, *Euripides V* (Chicago: University of Chicago Press, 1959), p. 53.

55. Force, p. 96.

56. Force, p. 124.

57. Joseph Campbell, *Primitive Mythology: The Masks of God* (New York: Penguin Books, 1987), p. 4.

58. Euripides' *Orestes*, pp. 310 and 313.

59. William Shakespeare, *Hamlet*, ed. Louis B. Wright (New York: Washington Square Press, 1958), p. 29.

60. Euripides' *Orestes*, p. 337.

IV

61. L. C. Knight, *Drama and Society in the Age of Jonson* (London: Chatto & Windus, 1962).

62. Woodbridge, p. 55.

63. Woodbridge, p. 56.

64. Woodbridge, p. 61.

65. Woodbridge, p. 67.

66. Woodbridge, p. 68.

67. William Shakespeare, *Hamlet* (New York: Washington Square Press, 1958), p. 82. There are numerous editions of Shakespeare. This edition was convenient for the author. However, for the convenience of the reader, quotations are accompanied by act, scene and line indications.

68. Susan Letzler Cole, *The Absent One* (University Park: Pennsylvania University Press, 1985), p. 51.

69. Peter Brook, *The Empty Space* (New York: Atheneum, 1984), p. 56.

70. Cole, pp. 46-7.

71. Cole, pp. 51, 46-7 and 5.

72. Cole, p. 5.

73. Kott, pp. 252-3 and 257-8.

74. Kott, pp. 254 and 253.

75. Cole, p. 11.

V

76. Lilian Feder, *Madness in Literature* (Princeton, N.J.: Princeton University Press, 1980).

77. See Carl E. Schorske, *Fin de-Siècle Vienna* (New York: Vintage Books, 1981).

78. Schorske, p. 186.

79. Quoted in Schorske, p. 194.

80. Schorske; the quotations are from pp. 196, 197, 197, 199 and 203, respectively.

81. Oscar Wilde, *Salome*, in *The Complete Works of Oscar Wilde* (New York: Harper and Row, 1966), p. 319. Hereafter, quotations of this edition are indicated with page number references in parentheses or brackets.

82. Wilde, p. 328.

83. Schorske, p. 19.

84. Schorske, p. 19.

85. Schorske, p. 19.

86. Schorske, p. 21.

87. Hugo von Hofmannsthal, *Electra*, trans. Carl Richard Mueller, in *The Modern Theatre*, ed. Robert W. Corrigan (New York: Macmillan, 1964), p. 110. Hereafter, quotations from this edition are indicated by page number references in parenthesis or brackets.

88. David Cole, *The Theatrical Event* (Middletown, Conn.: Wesleyan University Press, 1975).

89. Hofmannsthal, p. 114.

90. Suzanne E. Bales, "Elektra: From Hofmannsthal to Strauss," doctoral diss., Stanford, 1984.

91. Levi-Strauss, p. 215.

92. Bales, p. 126.

93. Slater, p. 91.

94. Slater, p. 91.

95. Northrop Frye, *Anatomy of Criticism* (Princeton, N.J.: Princeton University Press, 1957), p. 217.

96. Hofmannsthal, p. 108.

97. Hofmannsthal, p. 90.

98. Hofmannsthal, p. 97.

99. Euripides. *Orestes and Other Plays* (Middlesex, England: Penguin Books, 1983), p. 310.

100. Eugene O'Neill, "Mourning Becomes Electra," in *Nine Plays* (New York: Modern Library, 1959), p. 739. Hereafter, quotations from this edition are indicated by page number references in parentheses or brackets.

101. Jean Giraudoux, *Electra*, in *Orestes and Electra*, ed. William M. Force (Boston: Houghton Mifflin, 1968), p. 138. Hereafter, quotations from this edition are indicated by page number references in parentheses or brackets.

102. Robert Cohen, *Giraudoux: Three Faces of Destiny* (Chicago: University of Chicago Press, 1968), p. 116.

103. Giraudoux, p. 148.

104. Cole, p. 142.

105. Lawrence Clark Powell, *Robinson Jeffers: The Man and His Work* (Los Angeles: Primavera Press, 1934), p. 13.

106. Powell, p. 14.

107. Powell, pp. 16 and 17 (emphasis added).

108. Louis Adamic, *Robinson Jeffers: A Portrait* (Seattle: University of Washington Chapbooks, 1929), pp. 33–4.

109. Robinson Jeffers, *The Tower Beyond Tragedy* in *The Selected Poetry of Robinson Jeffers* (New York: Random House, 1959), p. 138. Hereafter, quotations from this edition are indicated by page number references in parentheses or brackets.

110. Jeffers, p. 110.

111. Jeffers, p. 107.

112. René Girard, *Violence and the Sacred*, trans. Patrick Gregory (Baltimore: Johns Hopkins University Press, 1977), p. 49.

113. Girard, pp. 81–2.

VI

114. Peter Brook, *The Empty Space* (New York: Atheneum, 1984).

115. "*Electra*: Theater," *Downtown*, 2 Dec. 1987.

116. Ezra Pound, *Elektra*, trustees of the Ezra Pound Literary Property Trust, 1987, p. 72. Hereafter, quotations from this edition are indicated by page number references in parenthesis or brackets.

117. "Electra," rev. of *Elektra*, by Ezra Pound, dir. Carey Perloff, *Theater*, 2 Dec. 1987.

118. John Peter, "Why Broadway's Fairy-Tale Lacks a Happy Ending," rev. of *Elektra*, by Ezra Pound, dir. Carey Perloff, *The Sunday Times*, 8 Nov. 1987.

119. Jack Richardson, *The Prodigal*, in *Orestes and Electra*, ed. William M. Force (Boston: Houghton Mifflin, 1968), p. 211. Hereafter, quotations from this edition are indicated by page number references in parentheses or brackets.

120. Neumann, p. 190.

121. Adrienne Kennedy, *Electra*, in *In One Act* (Minneapolis: University of Minnesota Press, 1988), p. 105. Hereafter, quotations from this edition are indicated by an "E" and page number references in parentheses or brackets.

122. Euripides, *The Medea*, in *Euripides I*, ed. David Grene and Richmond Lattimore (Chicago: University of Chicago Press, 1955), p. 92.

123. Adrienne Kennedy, *Orestes*, in *In One Act* (Minneapolis: University of Minnesota Press, 1988), p. 147. Hereafter, quotations from this edition are indicated by an "O" and page number references in parentheses or brackets.

124. Simone de Beauvoir, *The Second Sex*, trans. and ed. H. M. Parshley (New York: Vintage Books, 1974), p. 202.

125. The Beauvoir quotations are, respectively, from pages 202, 165, 203 and 161.

126. Sue-Ellen Case, *Feminism and Theater* (New York: Methuen, 1988), p. 15.

127. Heiner Muller, *Hamlet-machine*, ed. Carl Weber (New York: Performing Arts Journal Publications, 1984), p. 53. Hereafter, quotations from this edition are indicated by page number references in parentheses or brackets.

128. Maria Ley Piscator, *The Piscator Experiment: The Political Theatre* (Edwardsville: Southern Illinois University Press, 1967).

129. Muller, p. 55.

VII

130. T. S. Eliot, *The Family Reunion* (New York: Harcourt Brace, 1939), pp. 21–2. Hereafter, quotations from this edition are indicated by page number references in parentheses or brackets.

131. Eliot, p. 32.

132. Sam Shepard, *Curse of the Starving Class*, in *Seven Plays* (New York: Bantam Books, 1986), p. 194. Hereafter, quotations from this edition are indicated by page number references in parentheses or brackets.

133. Shepard, pp. 157 and 150.

134. Shepard, pp. 155 and 153.

135. Shepard, pp. 196 and 196–7.

136. Shepard, p. 163.

Conclusion

137. Michael McLain, "The Directorial Challenge in New Technology," *New Theater*, 1985, p. 8/12.

138. McLain, pp. 7/11–9/13.

Bibliography

Ackerman, Roberts. *The Myth and Ritual School: J. G. Frazer and the Cambridge Ritualists*. New York: Garland Publishers, 1991.

Adam, Peter. *Art of the Third Reich*. (20th century German Art.) New York: H. N. Abrams, 1992. 322p.

Aeschylus. *The Oresteia*, trans. Robert Fagles. New York: Penguin Books, 1977. Fagles' translation was chosen for the relationship that he recognizes between the language of the play and that of the ancient myth of the death and rebirth of nature.

_____. *The Orestes Plays of Aeschylus*, trans. Paul Roche. New York: New American Library, 1962.

Ahlberg-Cornell, Gudrun. *Myth and Epos in Early Greek Art: Representation and Interpretation*. (Studies in Mediterranean Archeology.) Jonsered: P. Astoms Forlag, 1992. 410p.

Approaches to Greek Myth. Edited and introduced by Lowell Edmunds. Baltimore: Johns Hopkins University Press, 1990.

Aristotle. *Poetics*, trans. Gerald F. Else. Ann Arbor: University of Michigan Press, 1970. Authoritative modern reading, chosen for its clarity of language and its scholarly yet independent interpretation of Aristotle's ancient definition of theater.

Armstrong, Robert Plant. *Wellspring: On the Myth and Source of Culture*. Berkeley: University of California Press, 1975. Art and mythology, and psychological aspects of art.

Artaud, Antonin. *The Theater and Its Double*. New York: Grove Press, 1958. Artaud's theory of theater as a play of the volatile and the dangerous, as a magical and violent attack of theatrical images upon an audience is suggested in this work as part of its emerging definition of theater.

Auerback, Nina. *Women and the Demon: The Life of a Victorian Myth*. Cambridge, Mass.: Harvard University Press, 1982. Feminism in the literature of 19th century England.

Ausband, Stephen C. *Myth and Meaning, Myth and Order*. Macon, Ga: Mercer University Press, 1983.

Bachofen, Johan Jakob. *Myth, Religion, and Mother Right: Selected Writings of J. J. Bohofen*. Translated from the German by Ralph Manheim. Preface by George Boas. Introduction by Joseph Campbell. (Bollingen Series, 84.) Princeton, N.J.: Princeton University Press, 1967.

Bales, Suzanne E. "Elektra: From Hofmannsthal to Strauss." Diss. Stanford University, 1984.

Baring, Anne. *The Myth of the Goddess: Evolution of an Image*. Harmondsworth, England: Viking Arkana, 1991.

Barish, Jonas. *The Anti-Theatrical Prejudice*. Los Angeles: University of

California Press, 1981. A scholarly, detailed record of the antipathy toward theater that has been held by guardians of morality within Western history. This book is a record of the fear that the rational and the political have always felt for the passionate, the emotional and the theatrical.

Barksdale, E. C. *Cosmologies of Consciousness: Science and Literary Myth in an Exploration of the Beginnings and Development of Mind.* Cambridge, Mass.: Schenkman, 1980. Covers creative psychology and mythology.

Beauvoir, Simone de. *The Second Sex*, trans. and ed. H. M. Parshley. New York: Vintage Books, 1974. Beauvoir's work was the first and most important work on the psychology and nature of women within feminist literature. In a woman's voice it studies the historical, biological, psychological and sexual forces of femininity.

Beitl, Sheldon Jerome. "Hofmannsthal's 'Elektra' and O'Neil's 'Mourning Becomes Electra': The Nature of Life." Diss. California State University, 1977.

Bentley, Eric. *The Life of the Drama.* New York: Atheneum Press, 1983. Authoritative study of the dynamics of theater written by one of the giants of modern theater-criticism.

_____. *The Pirandello Commentaries.* Evanston, Ill.: Northwestern University Press, 1986. A series of essays on the theatricality within the plays of Pirandello, this slim book recognizes Pirandello as the herald of modern theater.

Biological Woman — The Convenient Myth: A collection of Feminist Essays and a Comprehensive Bibliography, ed. Ruth Hubbard, Mary Sue Henifin and Barbara Fried. Cambridge, Mass.: Schenkman, 1902. Deals with feminism, discrimination against women, and sex roles.

Black, Katherine C. "Direct Address In Sophocles: A Study in Dramatic Convention." Diss. Catholic University of America, 1985. Covers a variety of topics, including stagecraft, marked and unmarked words, power and solidarity, and vocatives.

Blau, Herbert. *Blooded Thought.* New York: Performing Arts Journal Publications, 1982. One of the most authoritative theater-scholars of our time, Blau combines academic inquiry with the practical experience of the director. This book is a dynamic study of theater-in-practice and of the risks that it demands.

_____. *Take Up the Bodies: Theater at the Vanishing Point.* Chicago: University of Illinois Press, 1982. Included here for its sense that theater is an attempt to capture past dreams and hold them in the present, an attempt to envision a better future based on some half recalled utopia, i.e: theater as the recapturing of myth.

Blundell, Mary Whitlock. "Sophocles: An Ethical Approach. A Study of 'Electra,' 'Philoctetes' and 'Oedipus at Colonus'." Diss. University of California, Berkeley, 1981.

Brecht, Bertolt. *Collected Plays*, ed. Ralph Manheim. New York: Vintage Books, 1971.

Brook, Peter. *The Empty Space.* New York: Atheneum, 1984. Seminal work on theory-criticism by the great director. A definition of "live" theater.

_____. *The Shifting Point.* New York: Harper & Row, 1987. A series of brilliant essays in which Brook talks about his innovative work as director. Includes his dynamic treatment of Shakespeare, of opera and of film.

Brustein, Robert. *The Theatre of Revolt*. Boston: Atlantic Monthly Press, 1964. A series of essays on theater as the act of rebellion, covering the works of the founders of modern theater: Ibsen, Strindberg, Chekhov, Shaw, Brecht, Pirandello, O'Neill and Genet.

Buller, Jeffrey Lynn. "Sophocles and the Sacred Hero." Diss. University of Wisconsin, Madison, 1981.

Burgess, Dana Livingston. "Late Euripidean Narrative." Diss. Bryn Mawr College, 1984.

Burkert, Walter. *Ancient Mystery Cults*. Cambridge, Mass.: Harvard University Press, 1987. Four chapters, developed out of four lectures given at Harvard University in 1982. A graphic, documented description of these ancient cults.

Campbell, Joseph. *The Hero with a Thousand Faces*. Princeton, N.J.: Princeton University Press, 1968. This classic work examines the "hero" within myths from all regions of the world and relates their stories to the vision of the prophets of world religions, such as Moses, Jesus and Mohammed, and to dreams recorded in clinical studies, by modern psychoanalysts. From this the great master of mythology extracts a prototype: the archetypal hero.

_____. *Primitive Mythology: The Masks of God*. New York: Penguin Books, 1987. Authoritative study in which Campbell reads ancient world mythology, its symbols and its meanings, from the modern perspectives of archeology, anthropology and psychology.

Case, Sue-Ellen. *Feminism and Theater*. New York: Methuen Press, 1988. In this slim book Case deconstructs male-oriented theater and the male perspective, and introduces the female aesthetic.

Clemon-Karp, Sheila. "The Female Androgyne in Tragic Drama." Diss. Brandeis University, 1980. A redefinition of the "female" and the "feminine" in tragic drama.

Cohen, Sandra Heiman. "The Electra Figure in Twentieth Century American and European Drama." Diss. Indiana University, 1969.

Cole, David. *The Theatrical Event*. Middletown, Conn.: Wesleyan University Press, 1975. A study of theater as an altered state, as one in which the unphysical, i.e. the life within the mind, is encapsulated, for the theatrical moment, within physical form. All aspects of the theater are scrutinized from this perspective.

Cole, Susan Letzler. *The Absent One: Mourning, Ritual, Tragedy and the Performance of Ambivalence*. University Park, Pa.: Pennsylvania State University Press, 1985. In this scholarly and erudite examination of classical texts, Cole discovers a similar acting-out of ambivalent impulses within funeral rites and tragic drama.

Corrigan, Robert Willoughby. "The 'Electra' Theme in the History of Drama." Diss. University of Minnesota, 1955.

Crane, Walter. *Echoes of Hellas: The Tale of Troy and the Story of Orestes from Homer and Aeschylus*. London: M. Ward, 1887–1888. Presented in 82 designs with introductory essay and sonnets by George G. Warr.

Diggle, James. *The Textual Tradition of Euripides' Orestes*. New York: Oxford University Press, 1991.

Dinerstein, Norman Myron. "Polychordality in 'Salome' and 'Elektra': A Study of the Application of Reinterpretation Technique." Diss. Princeton University, 1974.

Durry, Marie-Jeanne. *L'Univers de Giraudoux*. France: Mercure de France Press, 1961. In this slim volume, Durry depicts Giraudoux as a man who is torn between the conflicting loyalties of France and Germany in World War II.

Eden, Kathy Hannah. "The Influence of Legal Procedure on the Development of Tragic Structure." Diss. Stanford University, 1980. Studies the origins and development of the tragic form in drama with an examination of both the literary and critical conditions of fifth-century Athens, early Imperial Rome and Elizabethan England.

Eliade, Mircea. *The Myth of the Eternal Return*. Princeton, N.J.: Princeton University Press, 1974. Authoritative scholarship on the world of the ancients.

_____. *Shamanism*. Princeton, N.J.: Princeton University Press, 1974. Authoritative source.

Eliot, T. S. *The Family Reunion*. New York: Harcourt Brace Jovanovich, 1939.

Esslin, Martin. *An Anatomy of Drama*. New York: Hill and Wang, 1976.

Euripides. *Euripides I*, ed. David Grene and Richmond Lattimore. Chicago: University of Chicago Press, 1955.

_____. *Orestes and Other Plays*, trans. Philip Vellacott. Middlesex: Penguin Books, 1983. Chosen for its reliability and clarity.

_____. *Ten Plays*, trans. Moses Hadas and John McLean. New York: Bantam Books, 1985. Chosen for its modern translation of *Hyppolytus* and for the clear way in which it illustrates points discussed in the present work.

Feder, Lilian. *Madness in Literature*. Princeton, N.J.: Princeton University Press, 1980. A scholarly questioning of the human propensity for chaos, from its first traces in prehistoric times.

Foucault, Michel. *The History of Sexuality*, trans. Robert Hurley. New York: Vintage Books, 1980. A short, incisive discourse on the power and the politics of sexual behavior in Western civilization.

Freud, Sigmund. *Civilization and Its Discontents*. New York: W. W. Norton, 1961. This tiny book (104 pages) is Freud's masterpiece. It contains his most profound theories of human behavior, of Western civilization. According to Freud, the emancipation of the instincts necessary for the well-being of the individual is in direct conflict with the needs of society. Survival of society necessitates the repression of the individual.

Frost, Christopher Powell. "The Euripidean Recognition: A Study in Dramatic Form." Diss. University of Cincinnati, 1980.

Frye, Northrop. *The Anatomy of Criticism*. Princeton, N.J.: Princeton University Press, 1957.

Fuentes, Orlirio. "El Teatro de Virgilio Pinera." Diss. City University of New York, 1985.

Gaster, Theodor H. *Sacred Narrative*. Berkeley: University of California Press, 1984.

Gillian, Bryan Randolph. *Richard Strauss' Elektra*. New York: Oxford University Press, 1991.

Girard, Rene. *Violence and the Sacred*. Baltimore: Johns Hopkins University Press, 1977.

Giraudoux, Jean. *Electra, Stuck in zwei Akten*, trans. into German by Hans Rothe. Munich: List, 1959.

Goethe, Johann Wolfgang von. *Faust*, trans. Walter Arndt, ed. Cyrus Hawlin. New York: W. W. Norton, 1976.

Gordon, Bill. Review of *Elektra*, by Ezra Pound, dir. Carey Perloff. *Town & Village*, 12 Nov. 1987.

Grant, Michael. *The Rise of the Greeks*. New York: Macmillan, 1987.

Graves, Robert. *The White Goddess*. New York: Farrar, Straus and Giroux, 1948.

Grote, Dale Allan. "Sophocles' 'Electra': Social Document of Late Fifth Century Athens (Greece)." Diss. University of Wisconsin, Madison, 1990.

Grotowski, Jerzy. *Towards a Poor Theater*. New York: Simon & Schuster, 1968.

Grubb, Kevin. Review of *Elektra*, by Ezra Pound, dir. Carey Perloff. *New York Native*, 30 Nov. 1987.

Gussow, Mel. "Stage: Pound's 'Elektra'," rev. of *Elektra*, by Ezra Pound, dir. Carey Perloff. *New York Times*, 11 Nov. 1987.

Hauser, Arnold. *Mannerism: The Crisis of the Renaissance and the Origin of Modern Art*. Cambridge, Mass.: Belknap Press of Harvard University Press, 1986.

Hawkins, Jocelyn Hunter. "Hofmannsthal's 'Electra': The Play and the Opera." Diss. 1971.

Hechler, Marilyn E. "Past and Present in American Drama: The Case of Eugene O'Neill and Sam Shepard." Diss. State University of New York at Stony Brook, 1989. Chapter 3 discusses *Mourning Becomes Electra* and *Buried Child*. This study treats the paradoxial relationship of the myth with the naturalistic portrayal of the characters.

Hillman, James. *Anima: An Anatomy of a Personified Notion*. Dallas: Spring Publication, 1985.

_____. *Archetypal Psychology: A Brief Account*. Dallas: Spring Publications, 1981.

Hoffer, Stanley. "Audience Expectation in Greek Tragedy: Scenic Structures and Conflicts of Sympathies in Four Plays." Diss. University of California, Berkeley, 1993. Plays by Euripides and Sophocles.

Hofmannsthal, Hugo Von. "Electra," trans. Carl Richard Mueller in *The Modern Theater*, Robert Corrigan, ed. New York: Macmillan, 1964.

Homer. *The Odyssey: The Story of Odysseus*, trans. W. H. D. Rouse. New York: New American Library, 1937.

Jarry, Alfred. *Nihilism and the Theater of the Absurd*, ed. Maurice Marc Labelle. New York: New York University Press, 1980.

Jaeger, Werner. *Paideia: The Ideals of Greek Culture*, trans. Gilbert Highet. New York: Oxford University Press, 1965.

Jeffers, Robinson J. "The Tower Beyond Tragedy," in *Selected Poems*. New York: Random House, 1965.

Jung, C. G. *Four Archetypes: Mother/Rebirth/Spirit/Trickster.* Princeton, N.J.: Princeton University Press, 1959.
_____. *A Primer of Jungian Psychology.* New York: New American Library, 1973.
_____. *Symbols of Transformation.* Princeton, N.J.: Princeton University Press, 1956.
Kaplan, Howard Gary. "Borderline and Narcissistic Rage and Emptiness: Their Dramatization and Drama Therapy." Diss. Northwestern University, 1990. A psychological study of the myth of Orestes and Electra; deals with borderline personality disorder.
Kaplan, Richard Andrew. "The Musical Language of 'Elektra': A Study in Chromatic Harmony." Diss. University of Michigan, 1985. A musical investigation of Richard Strauss' *Elektra.*
Kennedy, Adrienne. *Adrienne Kennedy in One Act.* Minneapolis: University of Minnesota Press, 1988.
Kerr, Walter. *Tragedy and Comedy.* New York: Da Capo Press, 1985.
Kitto, H. D. F. *The Greeks.* New York: Penguin Books, 1986.
Kling, Vincent. "The Artist as Austrian: Social Principle in Some Early Works of Hugo Von Hofmannsthal." Diss. Temple University, 1990.
Knight, L. C. *Drama and Society in the Age of Jonson.* London: Chatto & Windus, 1962.
Kott, Jan. *The Eating of the Gods.* Evanston, Ill.: Northwestern University Press, 1973.
Lee-Bonanno, Lucy. "The Quest for Authentic Personhood: An Expression of the Female Tradition in Novels by Moix, Tusquets, Matute and Alos." Diss. University of Kentucky, 1984. Feminism in Catalonia.
Lefkowitz, Mary R., and Fant, Maureen B. *Women's Life in Greece and Rome: A Source Book in Translation.* Baltimore: Johns Hopkins University Press, 1977.
Levi-Strauss, Claude. *Structural Anthropology.* New York: Basic Books, 1963.
Lindemann, Louise Jeanne. "In Quest of Orestes: A Critical Study of the Figure in Dramas Ancient and Modern Dealing with the Orestes-Electra Legend." Diss. New York University, 1978.
Lois, Mary. "Becoming a Heroine: A Study of the Electra Theme." Diss. University of California, Riverside, 1984.
Maufort, Marc Jean. "Visions of the American Experience: The O'Neill-Melville Connection." Diss. Free University of Brussels, Belgium, 1986.
McDonald, Lawrence Francis. "Compositional Procedures in Richard Strauss' 'Electra'." Diss. University of Michigan, 1976.
Mclain, Michael. "The Directorial Challenge in New Technology." *New Theater,* I (1987) 7/11–9/13.
Muller, Heiner. *Hamlet-Machine,* ed. Carl Weber. New York: Performing Arts Journal Publications, 1984.
Murray, Gilbert. *Hamlet and Orestes: A Study in Traditional Types.* (British Academy, Annual Shakespeare Lecture, 1914.) New York: Oxford University Press, 1914.
Nelsen, Don. "Electrifying 'Elektra'," rev. of *Elektra,* by Ezra Pound, dir. Carey Perloff. *Daily News,* 16 Nov. 1987.

Neumann, Erich. *The Archetypal World of Henry Moore*. Princeton, N.J.: Princeton University Press, 1959.

──────. *Art and the Creative Unconscious*. Princeton, N.J.: Princeton University Press, 1959.

──────. *The Great Mother*. Princeton, N.J.: Princeton University Press, 1963.

──────. *The Origins and History of Consciousness*. Princeton, N.J.: Princeton University Press, 1954.

Nietzsche, Friedrich Wilhelm. *The Portable Nietzsche*, ed. Walter Kaufmann. New York: Penguin Books, 1959.

O'Neill, Eugene. *Nine Plays*. New York: Modern Library, 1959.

──────. *Three Plays of Eugene O'Neill*. New York: Vintage Books, 1952.

Ormand, Kirk W. B. "The Representation of Marriage in Sophoclean Drama." Diss. Stanford University, 1992. Feminist theory.

Paul, Angus. "World Premiere Focuses Long-Overdue Attention on Pound's Version of Sophocles's 'Elektra'," rev. of *Elektra*, by Ezra Pound, dir. Carey Perloff. *Chronicle of Higher Education*, 16 Dec. 1987.

Peter, John. "Why Broadway's Fairy-Tale Lacks a Happy Ending," rev. of *Elektra*, by Ezra Pound, dir. Carey Perloff. *Sunday Times*, 8 Nov. 1987.

Piscator, Maria Ley. *The Piscator Experiment: The Political Theatre*. Edwardsville, Ill.: Southern Illinois University Press, 1967.

Powell, Brenda Joyce. "The Metaphysical Quality of the Tragic: A Study of Sophocles' 'Electra,' Giraudoux' 'Electra' and Sartre's 'Les Mouches'." Diss. University of North Carolina at Chapel Hill, 1981.

Ridgeway, William. *The Origin of Tragedy*. New York: Benjamin Blom, 1966.

Ringer, Mark Justin. "Electra and the Empty Urn: A Study of Sophoclean Metatheatre." Diss. University of California, Santa Barbara, 1983.

Roheim, Geza. *The Gates of the Dream*. New York: International Universities Press, 1952.

Sacred Narrative: Readings in the Theory of Myth, ed. Alan Dundes. Berkeley: University of California Press, 1984.

Schechner, Richard. *Between Theater and Anthropology*. Philadelphia: University of Pennsylvania Press, 1985.

Schmitt, Patrick E. "'The Fountain,' 'Marco Millions,' and 'Lazarus Laughed': O'Neill's 'Exotics' as History Plays." Diss. University of Wisconsin, Madison, 1985.

Schorske, Carl E. *Fin-de-Siècle Vienna: Politics and Culture*. New York: Vintage Books, 1979.

Shakespeare, William. *Hamlet*. New York: Washington Square Press, 1958.

Shepard, Sam. *Seven Plays*. New York: Bantam Books, 1986.

Simpson, Paula. "A Response to the Ironic Reading of Sophocles' 'Electra'." Diss. Dalhousie University, 1991.

Slater, Philip E. *The Glory of Hera*. Boston: Beacon Press, 1968.

Smith, Louise Pearson. "Studies of Characterization in Euripidos: The 'Medeia,' 'Elektra,' and 'Orestes'." Diss. Princeton University, 1976.

Solmsen, Friedrich. *Electra and Orestes: Three Recognitions in Greek Tragedy*. Amsterdam: Noord-Hollandsche, 1967.

Song, Nina. *Death in the Tragedies of William Shakespeare and Eugene O'Neill*. Diss. State University of New York at Albany, 1988. Themes of

life-in-death, death-in-love, and love-as-death. Among the plays dealt
with in this collection are *Hamlet* and *Mourning Becomes Electra*.

Sophocles. *Electra and Other Plays*, trans. E. F. Watling. New York: Penguin
Books, 1978.

―――――. *Orestes and Electra*, ed. William M. Force. Boston: Houghton
Mifflin, 1968. This edition was chosen for its clarity of style and because
it best illustrates arguments used in the present work.

Soulis, Timothy Charles. "The Double Identity Pattern: Reality and Theatre
in the Characters of Sophocles, Shakespeare and Ibsen." Diss. University
of Denver, 1980.

Sroka, Elliott Frank. "The Other Side of Experience: The Radical Theater of
Euripides." Diss. Stanford University, 1980. This study compares the radical form of Euripides with those of Bertolt Brecht and Eugene Ionesco.

Strauss, Richard. *Elektra*, ed. Derrick Puffett. New York: Cambridge University Press, 1989.

Swart, Gerhardus Jacobus. "The Electra of Sophocles: A Critical Evaluation of
the Different Interpretations." Diss. University of Pretoria, South Africa,
1983.

Symanski, Leonard L. "Sign and Symbol in the Theater of Jean Giraudoux."
Diss. Middlebury College, 1982. French text.

Tripp, Edward. *The Meridian Handbook of Classical Mythology*. New York:
New American Library, 1970.

Tuck, Susan. "The O'Neill-Faulkner Connection." Diss. University of Indiana,
1984.

Turner, Victor. *From Ritual to Theatre: The Human Seriousness of Play*. New
York: PAJ Publications, 1982.

Van Gennep, Arnold. *The Rites of Passage*. Chicago: University of Chicago
Press, 1960.

Vernant, Jean-Pierre. *The Origins of Greek Thought*. Ithaca, N.Y.: Cornell
University Press, 1962.

Verrall, Arthur Woollgar. *Essays on Four Plays of Euripides: Andromache,
Helen, Heracles, Orestes*. New York: Cambridge University Press, 1905.

Wellein, Lawrence Theodore. "Time Past and the Hero: A Suggested Criterion
for Sophoclean Tragedy as Exemplified by the 'Ajax,' 'Traohiniao' and
'Electra'." Diss. University of Washington, 1969.

Wilde, Oscar. *The Complete Plays of Oscar Wilde*. New York: Harper & Row,
1966.

―――――. *Plays*. New York: Penguin Books, 1985.

Woodard, Thomas Marion. "'Elektra' by Sophocles: The Dialectical Design."
Diss. Harvard University, 1962.

Woodbridge, Linda. *Women and the English Renaissance*. Chicago: University
of Illinois Press, 1986.

Yunis, Harvey Evan. "Athenian Polis Religion and Euripides: Fundamental
Religious Beliefs in Life and Fiction." Diss. Harvard University, 1987.

Index